CANNING MEAT COOKBOOK FOR BEGINNERS

RAYMOND L HILLMAN

TABLE OF CONTENTS

CHAPTER 6
VENISON & RABBIT

CHAPTER 7
CHICKEN & TURKEY

CHAPTER 8
SOUPS, STOCKS AND BROTHS

CHAPTER 9
SOUP & SAUCE BASE RECIPES FOR ANY MEAT

CANNING MEAT COOKBOOK FOR BEGINNERS

CHAPTER 1
THE CURIOUS ORIGINS OF CANNING

We are so used to being able to preserve our food by canning. We never stop to think about what we would do if we weren't able to keep a wide stock of food supplies at home. Having a can or jar of food to reach out for is so convenient. It's invaluable! After all, processing and sealing food in airtight containers can increase its lifespan from 1 to 5 years. But let's go back to a time before canning. How did come in to being and why?

Well, its origins lie with the French. In Napoleonic times, a reward was offered by the French government to an inventor who could come up with an idea for preserving large quantities of food for the armies. So, in 1809, a clever French confectioner named Nicolas Appert discovered that food sealed in jars lasts for extended periods. Although he did not understand why this happened, he was awarded a 12,000-franc award and has since been nicknamed 'The Father of Food Science'. It wasn't until some 50 years later that Louis Pasteur discovered the role that microbes play in the safe and extended life of food stored in jars.

After the Napoleonic wars, canned food quickly took off in Europe and the US. In the US, the first canning factory was established in New York in 1812 (the house of Appert). Consumers enjoyed the fact that it was the cheapest and easiest method to store foods. The use of jars to preserve foods was reserved for more expensive items and is still the popular choice for home canning methods today.

Pressure cookers known as 'canner retorts' were manufactured for commercial use from 1905 by National Presto Industries. The company went from producing 50- gallon canners to 30-gallon canners for hotels, the 10-gallon ones for us in the home. In 1915 the company installed an aluminum foundry to enable the manufacturing of large-size pressure canners for home use.

The company made the move to cater to the home rather than the commercial market when the U.S. Department of Agriculture in 1917 announced that to enable the canning of low-acid foods without risking food poisoning, the only safe method was by pressure canning. In 1925 the company changed its name to the National Pressure Cooker Company, becoming the largest manufacturer in the world.

Today, the two methods for processing foods using heat are water bathing and pressure canning. Water bathing is where foods that have a high acidic level, (Ph 1.0-4.6) such as apples/strawberries can be processed safely using boiling water temperature of 212 degrees F/100 degrees C. This will destroy any microorganisms that could be harmful. Pressure canning is where foods that have a low/zero acidity level (pH 4.6/14.0) such as root vegetables or meats require the increased temperature that can be achieved with the pressure cooker, 240 degrees F/116 degrees C or more to enable harmful microorganisms to be destroyed.

So now we will dive into the world of pressure canning to preserve foods in your home that can be prepared, stored, and consumed later. We will mostly look at preserving meats (on their own or as part of a whole meal) but also soups, stocks, and broths so that you have a wide selection to prepare for your pantry.

BENEFITS OF CANNING MEAT

So why can meat? There are several reasons why canning and preserving meat is a great option for those who wish to be prepared and have delicious meals or meats to add to recipes whenever they wish.

1. **It's simple**- the art of canning and preserving meats is a simple process that we can all do for our families in the comfort of our own homes. With the addition of a pressure canner, I will show you how.
2. **It doesn't need electricity**- If you live out in the sticks, and have a non-dependable electricity supply, then canning some of your meat supply for your family is a clever move.
3. **It softens the meat**- By adding the meat to a pressure canner, (like cooking it for an extended time) the meat will become soft and succulent, ideal for many tasty recipes.
4. **You save on freezer space**- This space can then be used for the storage

of foods that cannot be prepared in the pressure canner or if you have a power cut then your meat supply is safe.

5. **No thawing required**- the advantage of canning meat is that it is readily available to use in your recipe or the whole meal is in the jar for your family to enjoy with minimal preparation.

MEATS SUITABLE FOR CANNING

A wide variety of meats can be canned. These include beef, lamb, pork, venison, veal, mutton, moose, and bear.

And there are more: poultry and game can be canned such as turkey, chicken, rabbit, goose, and duck.

We've also got some recipes for pressure canning soups, stews, and broths which in themselves make great delicious nutritious meals or add flavor to other dishes.

OTHER FOODS SUITABLE FOR CANNING

The following foods require canning in a pressure canner as they have a low acidity level (those with a Ph greater than 4.6), which means that they need the high temperatures reached by a pressure canner to make sure that they are preserved safely. Please follow your manufacturer's recommendations when canning the following products.

- Meat and vegetable stocks and broths
- Vegetables- green beans, pumpkin, potatoes, mushrooms, onions, and peppers
- Soups and stews
- Chili
- Baked beans
- Dry beans- pinto beans, black beans, navy beans, etc
- Pasta sauces containing low-acidic vegetables

FOODS THAT CANNOT BE PRESSURE CANNED

The following foods cannot be pressure canned as it would be unsafe to do so.

- Milk, butter, cream, and other dairy products
- Flour, corn starch, and most thickeners
- Coconut milk
- Starchy foods including rice and pasta
- Eggs (normal and pickled)

Milk and other dairy products are not suitable for canning as they have a low acidity level, and their fat content can protect and insulate clostridium botulinum (a foodborne illness-causing bacteria linked to home canning). During the process of canning, this bacterium would not be destroyed.

With eggs, the level of heat and length of time within a pressure canner is too much for eggs due to how sensitive and unpredictable they are. They would become rubbery and inedible.

CHAPTER 2
GETTING TO KNOW YOUR PRESSURE CANNER

Using a pressure canner is your safest way to can meat as it reaches temperatures above 240 degrees F/115.6 degrees C. A favourite in the 1970s, most pressure cookers now have been redesigned for today's fast-moving market. They are now lightweight, with thin walls and have turn-on lids complete with gaskets. In order to choose a safe pressure canner for home use, select one that has been approved by the Underwriter's Laboratory (UL).

Pressure canners are available in two forms: a weighted-gauge canner, which indicates and regulates the pressure or a dial-gauge pressure canner which indicates the pressure.

Follow the instructions to understand the specifics of your canner but weighted canners are generally designed to rock gently or jiggle a few times per minute to enable them to keep the desired pressure. This will vary from machine to machine so is important to know your canner well before use.

For dial-gauge canners to be pressurized, they either have a counterweight or a pressure regulator for sealing off the open vent. The pressure in the canner can be read on the dial.

Pressure canners can either hold a single layer of quart or smaller jars or can hold two layers of pint or smaller jars. For a canner to be considered a pressure canner it should be able to hold at least 4-quart jars.

Although instructions should be studied for your pressure canner before use, below are some instructions on how to successfully pressure can.

1. Ensuring that your canner is functioning properly is a good place to start. Make sure that all parts are clean, including the lid and gaskets, and that the vent pipes are clear. The range that your canner sits on must be level and the burner must give off the correct heat for your canner. Add the water and the rack into the canner. The water should be at a depth of 2-3

inches if it doesn't specify for your chosen food. More water may be required for particular foods such as smoked fish therefore always check your instructions before you start.

The water in the canner needs to be heated to 180 degrees F/82.2 degrees C for hot-packed foods (check to ensure the water level remains at the 2–3-inch depth) and for raw-packed foods, the water needs to be heated to 140 degrees F/60 degrees C.

2. Using a jar lifter, place the jars filled with the meat/soup/broth etc on the jar rack in the canner, ensuring the correct fitting of the lids with the ring bands. Always make sure the jar is kept upright to avoid any spillages of food into the sealing area of the lid.

3. Secure the lid on the canner and either open the petcock or leave the weight off the vent pipe.

4. Turn on the heat until the water boils and the steam flows for around 10 minutes from the open vent pipe or petcock.

5. Close the petcock or place the counterweight or weighted gauge on the vent pipe. It will take around 3 to 10 minutes for the canner to pressurize.

6. When the desired pressure is reached, the timing of the process can begin. This can be determined either by the reading on the dial gauge or when the weighted gauge begins to 'jiggle' as per instructions.

7. Maintain the heat under the canner to ensure the correct pressure. This will ensure that the food is processed safely and that there is no loss of liquid from the jars. If there is a drop in the pressure, then bring the canner back to the desired pressure and start the timer from the beginning to ensure the food has been processed properly.

8. Once the canning process is finished then turn off the heat and leave the canner in situ to allow it to cool down. The canner will also lose its pressure whilst it is cooling. Allow these two things to occur in their own time. Using cold water on the canner exterior or opening the vent pipe before it has depressurized will result in the jars losing liquid, and failure of the seals and may also damage the lid of the canner. Although measures are in place, please take care when removing the weight from the vent pipe in case there is any steam left in the system meaning it hasn't fully depressurized. This could lead to harm. New pressure canners have a cover lock or handle that must be released before the lids can be removed.

9. Wait for 10 mins after you have removed the weight from the vent pipe

or opened the petcock before you remove the lid and always lift the lid away from your face to avoid any potential burns.

10. Remove the jars, one at a time with a jar lifter, transferring them onto a cooling rack. Leave a space in between each jar.

11. Allow 12-24 hours for the jars to cool properly before tightening the ring bands or pushing down on the center of the lids.

12. The ring bands can then be removed from the sealed jars and washed for re-use. Any jars that have not been properly sealed will have to be stored in the refrigerator and the contents used as soon as possible.

13. Label all the sealed jars with the date processed and its contents and store them out of direct light in a cool, dry place.

14. The gasket, lid, and canner will need to be dried, and remove the pet-cocks and safety valves and wash and dry them. Each canner will come with its own set of instructions particular to that model. Please adhere to these to ensure the longevity of your canner and the successful and safe processing of foods within your canner.

Two of the most common makes of canners used today are:

- **Presto Pressure Canners**- a dial gauge canner that is good for those new to canning, it is cheap, and readily available. The disadvantage with these is that it takes a bit of practice to ensure the stove is at the correct temperature to maintain the required pressure of your canner for its contents and as the gaskets are constructed from rubber, they will require replacing at intervals.

- **All American Pressure Canners-** a weighted gauge pressure canner that is easy to use and lasts a long time. They can process larger quantities during one session and have no gaskets or seals to replace.

CHAPTER 3
HOW TO CAN BEEF, PORK, LAMB, VENISON AND MORE

When it comes to canning meats in your pressure canner it is best to follow the *raw* or *hot pack* methods.

Hot pack method: this is where you cook the meat before it is jarred. The meat does not need to be fully cooked but merely browned in a pan of oil before packing into the jars. Cooking the meat, causes it to reduce in size, therefore allowing you to pack more meat into each jar. It can also lengthen the storage time of the meat.

Raw pack method: you simply pack the meat into the jars whilst raw, saving you from spending time cooking the meat.

THE RAW PACK METHOD

Preparing the meat: Clean your meat by removing any connective tissue or excess fat that you do not wish to eat. Remove any meat from the bone. Cut the meat into cubes of a uniform size of around an inch.

Adding the meat to the jars: Start by washing the quart jars or pints and preparing the lids and rings. Fill each jar with the meat, packing it in well, making sure that you leave an inch free at the top of each jar.

Adding liquid to the jars: Some meats will create their own juices when pressure canned but some lean meats like venison will require additional fluid before processing. Here there are 3 options available:

- Add water to the jar
- Before putting the meat into the jar, add seasoning, chili flakes, etc, and then add the water
- Add stock or broth to your meat instead of water which will already contain seasoning

Use a bubble remover so that the liquid reaches the bottom of the jar. Check to ensure that the inch space is still visible. With a clean damp cloth, clean the rim of the jar and then close the jar with the lid and the ring.

Processing in the pressure canner: Place the jars in the pressure canner. With a presto canner add warm water to just below the band on the jars. Other pressure canners will not require this much liquid so please follow your manufacturer's instructions. Close the canner and turn the heat on high. It will take around 10-15 minutes for steam to start appearing. Set your timer for 10 minutes once the steam appears and allow the canner to vent. Then place the weight on the vent and watch the dial. The psi will vary according to your elevation so please follow the guidelines according to your altitude. For around 1000ft in elevation, the dial would need to reach 11 psi before the weight is put on the vent. The processing timer can then be started. Pint jars take around 75 minutes to process and quart jars around 90 minutes.

Storing canned meat: Turn off the heat and allow your canner to cool naturally. Once cooled, open the lid and leave the jars in the warm water for another 10 minutes. Remove the jars with a jar lifter, set them aside on a rack, and leave for around 12 hours. To check that the jars are properly sealed, press on the lid and if there is no movement then the procedure has been a success. Store the jars in your pantry after removing the rings. The meat within these jars will store for 2 years or more before consumption is necessary. When it comes to using the meat, it will be nicely softened and already seasoned for use in any dish of your choice to cook for your family. Pint jars are handy for a smaller-sized family.

THE HOT PACK METHOD

Preparing the meat: Trim off any excess fats and connective tissues and cut the meat into 1-inch cubes.

Browning the meat: Place the meat into a large pot and brown on both sides in a little oil or fat. It is not necessary to cook the meat all the way through.

Adding the meat to the jars: Add the meat to the freshly prepared jars leaving a 1-inch space at the top of each jar. Add 1 tsp of salt if you are using quart jars and ½ tsp of salt if using pint jars. The salt is added for flavor.

Adding liquid to the jars: Add water to the pot you browned the meat in and bring it up to a boil. This liquid will add extra flavor to your meat by adding this to your jars continuing to leave that 1-inch headroom.

Use your bubble remover so that the liquid reaches the bottom of your jars and with your clean damp cloth clean the rim of your jars and seal them with the lids and rings.

Processing in the pressure canner: Follow the guidelines of your canner for processing your jars. Around 10 psi is needed for 1000 ft above sea level. For pints will take around 75 minutes and for quarts around 90 minutes.

Storing canned meat: Remove your jars and allow them to cool as for the raw pack method above. Check the jars are sealed properly and store them for future use. The meat can simply be warmed and either eaten as it is or used in different stews, soups, and many other dishes.

HOW TO CAN POULTRY AND GAME

When it comes to processing poultry and game in your canner, although it can be done by using the raw pack method, it is sometimes easier to follow the hot pack method as when the meat is cooked it is easier to remove the meat from the bone and this makes for easier packing in the jars.

Preparing the poultry/game: Cook your chicken, turkey, or game in a pot for around 30-45 minutes or until the meat is soft and easily removed from the bones. Keep the liquid from the pot on one side. You can also use chicken breasts, thighs, legs, etc, cooked and cut into pieces, to add to your jars. Browning the meat in oil before canning adds and seals in the flavor or roasting in an oven increases the flavor significantly.

Adding the meat to the jars: Prepare the jars, lids, and rings making sure that they are clean. Pack the jars with the cooked meat leaving that 1-inch headspace. In your pressure canner, it is also good to add 2 inches of water and place it over high heat for the water to begin warming up ready for your jars.

Adding liquid to the jars: The liquid that the meat is cooked in is ideal for use in the jars as it is poultry/game stock already. Top up to leave that 1-inch space at the top of your jars. Water or store-bought stock can also be used here. Also, salt can be added at this point, which can preserve the taste. Add ½ tsp to a pint jar and 1 tsp to a quart jar. Seasoning can also be added. Just be aware that in a pressure canner flavor can intensify, so experiment and adjust to suit you and your family's taste.

Use your bubble remover to remove any air bubbles. With a clean cloth wipe the rim of your jars and then seal them with the lids and the rings.

Processing in the pressure canner: Place the jars on the rack in the canner which now contains the simmering water. Closing the canner and turning the heat up to high, wait for steam to be produced. Once steam begins to vent, set the timer for 10 minutes and the heat can be reduced during this period. The weight can then be placed on the vent. Watch the dial. Processing takes around 75 minutes for pint jars and around 90 minutes for quart jars. Again, the pressure will require adjustment according to your level of elevation and if you are using a weighted-gauge canner.

Storing canned poultry and game: When finished, turn off the heat and allow the canner to cool and depressurize. Remove the lids but leave the jars in the warm water for another 10 minutes. Remove the jars with your jar lifter and leave them to cool on a rack overnight. Check success by pressing on the center of the lids, removing the rings, and cleaning and storing them in your pantry. The meat inside is generally good for around a year to 18 months.

CHAPTER 4
FREQUENTLY ASKED QUESTIONS

1. **How do I know how much water I need to put in my canner for the process**?

Although you should check your canner's manufacturer's instructions, generally you will need to add around 2 inches to your canner. Once the jars are in the canner, check that the water level is not above their necks. If it is, then you must remove some of the water before processing.

2. **How do I vent my pressure canner?**

For pressure to build up safely in your canner, you must let out any extra air that is contained in the canner before you begin. This is done by using the steam vent. The steam escapes from your vent by removing the weight. Once the steam has started, wait 10 minutes before adding the weight to allow the pressure to build safely in your canner.

3. **How do I prevent my pressure canner from blowing up?**

Although modern pressure canners today have numerous built-in safety features, there are two things that you can do to avoid the danger of this ever occurring. These are:

- Ensure that your pressure canner is fitted with safety valves. Before any dangerous levels of pressure can occur within your canner these are designed to pop out.
- Check that the vent pipe is not blocked by removing the lid to see if you can see light shining through. If you can't see light, it will need to be cleaned.

4. **What adjustments need to be made to allow for the level of elevation?**

Based on your level of elevation, water will boil at different temperatures.

For your food within the canner to be able to reach a temperature of 240-250 degrees F/115.6-121.1 degrees C ensuring that it has been processed safely for storage, it will be necessary to add more pressure to your canner if you are at high elevations where the temperature will be lower.

For a weighted- gauge canner, you may need to add an additional 5 pounds of pressure. If using a dial-gauge canner you need to ensure that it is working properly by servicing it every year and this can be used to make small adjustments to your pressures. Most pressure canning recipes that you will follow will be based on a zero -1000ft. elevation so you will need to make some adjustments if you live at a different level. There are numerous tables that will serve you as a guide.

For an altitude of 1-1,000ft, you will require 10 psi for a weighted- gauge and 11 psi for a dial-gauge canner.

For an altitude of 1,001-2,000ft, you will require 15 psi for a weighted- gauge and 11 psi for a dial-gauge canner.

For an altitude of 2001-4,000ft, you will require 15 psi for a weighted- gauge and 12 psi for a dial-gauge canner.

For an altitude of 4,001-6,000ft, you will require 15 psi for a weighted- gauge and 13 psi for a dial-gauge canner.

For an altitude of 6,001-8,000ft, you will require 15 psi for a weighted gauge and 14 psi for a dial-gauge canner.

For an altitude of 8.001-10.000ft, you will require 15 psi for a weighted gauge and 15 psi for a dial-gauge canner.

5. What is the shelf life of a pressure-canned jar of food?

If a jar is sealed then the food inside should last for many years, but after a year, the food inside may begin to lose its flavor and its nutritional value. Therefore, rotating your pantry will ensure that you are always eating the best-tasting foods of the highest nutritional content.

WARNINGS! WHAT NOT TO DO WHEN PRESSURE CANNING!

1. **Don't be tempted to change the recipe**.

It is best to follow an approved recipe to avoid any food concerns after processing your jars/pints/quarts.

2. **Don't forget to get your dial-gauge tested every year.**

Incorrect readings result in food being canned wrongly, making it potentially harmful to consume. If you find this difficult to have it tested, then it may be worth buying a weighted-gauge canner instead.

3. **Don't overfill your canner**

When placing your jars in the canner make sure that it has only 2 inches of water in it before you begin. The water level should not be up to the necks of the jars.

4. **Don't fill your jars too high.**

For the jar to be properly sealed there needs to be at least a 1-inch space left at the top of the jar after filling. This space may vary according to your recipe but it's something to watch out for.

5. **Don't force cool your canner**

After the process, it takes a while for the canner to come down to room pressure before you can safely remove the jars. This process should not be quickened by attempting to force cool your canner or by releasing the pressure too quickly. You should not remove the weight, tap the jiggler or immerse your canner in cold water. This would cause the pressure to change suddenly leading to the cracking of the jars, ruining your seals, and ultimately damaging your pressure canner beyond use.

RECIPES
INTRODUCTION

Whether you are canning to help you manage your grocery shopping and budgeting, stockpiling for an emergency, or just want to stock your pantry for those days when you want home-cooked food to hand without the hassle of preparation – then these recipes will work for you.

With 52 main meat dish options and 28 soups, broths or stocks, choosing 1 of each per day would give you an incredible 364 days of different daily menus.

Our recipes typically make batches of 8-12 servings, so if you made every recipe, you would have enough servings for more than 2 years! Canned foods can even last up to 5 years, so with our canning recipes you can easily stock your pantry with incredible variety, ready to heat up whenever you want healthy food with that home-cooked taste.

So, now you can get started on the nutritious recipes that we have for you to try at home with your canner. Good luck and enjoy the process of preparing a variety of meals for you and your family.

IMPORTANT NOTE: These recipes give Guidelines for preparing food with typical canners but <u>always consult your manufacturer's specifications</u> on prepping your canner and jars, headspace, processing times, and pressure readings according to your altitudes.

CHAPTER 5
BEEF & PORK

1. STEWED BEEF AND VEGETABLES

A tasty stew packed full of flavor.

Prep time: 10 minutes
Cook time: 2hours 30 minutes
Makes: 10 servings

Ingredients

- 1-1 ½ lbs of stewing beef (cut into chunks)
- 1 cup onions (diced)
- 2 cups celery (diced)
- 1 cup carrots (peeled and sliced)
- 4 cups of potatoes (peeled and chopped)
- 1 tbsp vegetable oil (extra as required)
- 1 tsp dried thyme
- 1 tsp salt
- ½ tsp black pepper
- Boiling water

Method

1. Prepare your pressure canner, jars, and lids.
2. In a large pan heat the oil and brown the beef, portions at a time.
3. Transfer the beef to a large saucepan.
4. Add the potatoes, vegetables, thyme, seasonings, and boiling water and bring to a boil.
5. Move the stew to the jars, filling to within 1 inch of the top, and remove any air bubbles.
6. Dip a paper towel in vinegar and wipe the rim of each jar to remove any excess fat. Place the lid on the jar, and screw on the band.

7. Put the jars into the pressure cooker, lock the lid and bring to a boil.

8. Allow the steam to escape for 10 minutes. Process in accordance with your manufacturer's recommendations. As a guide for weighted gauge pressure canners- 75 minutes at 10lbs at sea level to 1000ft for pints and quarts 90 minutes. For dial gauge pressure canners 11 lbs of pressure at sea level to 2,000ft.

9. Allow the pressure to return to zero, wait for two minutes before opening the vent. Take off the pressure canners lid, wait 10 minutes and remove the jars. Allow cooling for 12 hours, check the seals, and label before storing.

2. CHILI CON CARNE

A firm family favorite to add to your rice

Process time: 75 minutes
Makes: 3 pints

Ingredients

- 1 lb ground beef
- 1 cup red kidney beans
- 2 cups of water
- ½ cup onion(chopped)
- 1/3 cup peppers (chopped)
- 1 ½ tsp salt
- 1/3 tsp pepper
- 1-2 tsp chili powder
- 4 cups tomatoes

Method

1. Wash and add the beans to a pan. Add cold water to cover the beans and soak for 12-18 hours.
2. Drain and add the 2 cups of water to the beans and add ½ tsp salt.
3. Bring up to boil, simmer for 30 minutes and drain.
4. In a pan brown the beef, onions, and peppers.
5. Drain the fat and add 1 tsp salt, kidney beans, tomatoes, chili powder, and pepper. Simmer for 5 minutes.
6. Leaving an inch free at the top of each jar, fill them with the mixture.

7. Please read your manufacturer's recommendations for process time in your specific pressure canner, but as a guide, in a dial-gauge pressure canner the process will take 75 minutes at 11lbs pressure at 0-2000ft altitude and 75 minutes at 10lbs pressure at 0-1,000 ft altitude in a weighted-gauge canner.
8. Remove the jars from the canner once cooled and de-pressurized and set aside to cool for 12 hours.
9. Check the jars are sealed, label them and place them in your pantry.

3. BEEF BOLOGNESE

This a tasty recipe to have with your spaghetti.

Process time: 60 minutes
Makes: 3 pints

Ingredients

- 1 lb ground beef
- 300g mushrooms (sliced)
- 2 garlic cloves (crushed)
- 1/3 cup green peppers (diced)
- 1/3 cup diced onions
- 10lbs tomatoes
- 1 1/3 tbsp parsley(minced)
- ¾ tbsp oregano
- 1 ½ tsp salt
- 1/8 cup brown sugar
- ¾ tsp black pepper

Method

1. Remove the skins from the tomatoes by immersing them in boiling water for around 30 seconds and transferring them to cold water.
2. Take out the tomato cores and cut them into quarters.
3. In a large pan cook for 20 minutes uncovered, then sieve.
4. Stir fry the beef in another pan until brown, then add the mushrooms, green peppers, onion, and garlic. Continue cooking until the vegetables are just softening.

5. Add the meat and vegetables to the saucepan with the tomatoes and mix well. Add the sugar, spices, and salt.
6. Bring this mixture to a boil, then uncover and simmer until the mixture thickens.
7. Transfer the mixture to your jars leaving an inch at the top and fix the lids on as recommended.
8. Process according to your manufacturer's recommendations but as a guide in a dial-gauge pressure canner it takes around 60 minutes at 11lb PSI at an altitude of 0-2000ft or in a weighted-gauge pressure canner it takes around 60 minutes at 10lb PSI at an altitude of 0-1000ft.
9. Remove the jars from your canner once cooled and de-pressurized and set aside to cool for 12 hours.
10. Check the jars are sealed, label them, and transfer them to your pantry.

4. POTTED BEEF (RAW PACKED)

A tender tasty meal to enjoy with your family.

Process time: 90 minutes
Makes: 8 quart jars

Ingredients

- 6 lbs chuck roast (cut into chunks)
- 4 cups beef broth
- 2 cups red wine
- 6 cups potatoes (peel and chopped)
- 4 cups carrots (peeled/sliced)
- 2 cups onions (chopped)
- 8 bay leaves
- 8 garlic cloves
- 4 tsp thyme(dried)
- 2 tsp black pepper
- 4 tsp salt

Method

1. Place 8 one-quart jars in your pressure canner along with a few inches of water and heat them until the water reaches 140 degrees F/60 degrees C.
2. Mix the wine and broth in a pan and bring to a boil. Then reduce to simmer.

3. Take the jars out of the pressure canner and add ¾ lb of raw meat into each jar along with ¼ cup of onions, ¾ cup of potatoes, and ½ cup of carrots.
4. Add 1 garlic clove, ½ tsp salt, ¼ tsp pepper, ½ tsp thyme, and a bay leaf to the jars.
5. Add the broth mixture to each jar until within an inch of the top, removing any air bubbles. Top up the jars if necessary.
6. Secure the lids on the jars (after wiping them) with the rings and return them to the canner.
7. Process as per manufacturer's recommendations, around 10 psi for 90 minutes.
8. Once processed and the canner has been left to lose its pressure, take out the jars and leave them on one side for 12 hours. This mixture will store well for up to a year.
9. To prepare for your family, transfer the jar's contents to a pan and bring it to a boil. Reduce the heat and add 1 tbsp flour for each quart jar to thicken the mixture. Stir gently and take out the bay leaf before serving this delicious meal to your family.

5. RED WINE BEEF

A delicious hearty meal when served with rice, noodles, or mashed potato.

Process time: 90 minutes
Makes: 8 quarts

Ingredients

- 4-5 oz. bacon(chopped)
- 4 ¼ lbs chuck beef (cubed)
- 4 ½ cups onions (chopped)
- 2 ¼ lbs mushrooms (sliced)
- 6 ¾ cups carrots (peeled and sliced)
- 2 ¼ cups red wine
- 16 cloves garlic (peeled and minced)
- 1-quart water

Method

1. Heat 8 jars in your pressure canner with a few inches of water and heat on the cooker until the water reaches 180 degrees F/82.2 degrees C.

2. Fry the bacon in a pot until it's crispy, remove, leaving the fat to fry the beef in. Once browned transfer to a container until all the meat portions are prepared.

3. Add the vegetables and garlic to the pot, then add the bacon, wine, and water. Bring up to a boil and simmer for a further 5 minutes.

4. Transfer the solid mixture to the jars and then top up to within 1 inch of the top of the jars with the broth.

5. Remove any air bubbles and top up if required.

6. Secure lids and transfer them for processing in your pressure canner.

7. Process as per your manufacturer's recommendations, but a guide is around 90 minutes at 10 psi depending on your altitude.

8. Remove the jars (after the pressure has been released) and leave to cool for 12 hours. Check the jars are sealed, label them, and transfer them to your pantry. Will store for up to 1 year.

9. To prepare for your family, pour the contents of the jar into a pot and heat for around 10 minutes. Stir whilst simmering and everything is thoroughly re-heated. Enjoy with rice, potatoes, or noodles.

6. FESTIVE PIE FILLING

A delicious pie filling, ideal for thanksgiving.

Process time: 90 minutes
Makes: 7 quarts

Ingredients

- 4 lbs ground beef (or 4 lbs venison and 1 lb sausage)
- 2 cups suet (chopped)
- 5 quarts apple (sliced)
- 2 quarts apple cider
- 5 cups of sugar
- 2 lbs dark raisins (seedless)
- 1 lb white raisins
- 2 tbsp ground cinnamon
- 2 tsp ground nutmeg
- 2 tbsp salt

Method

1. To avoid browning, cook the meat and suet in water.
2. Add the apples, suet, and meat to a food processor to blend.
3. In a pan add this mixture along with all the other ingredients and simmer for around 1 hour, stirring frequently, until the mixture is thickened.
4. Add the mixture to the jars leaving 1-inch clear at the top of each jar.
5. Fix the lids and bands and process in your canner.
6. For a dial-pressure canner for 0-2,000ft you will need a PSI of 11 lb and process for 90 minutes and for a weighted-gauge canner you will need a PSI of 10lb and process for 90 minutes.
7. Remove the jars from the canner once cooled and de-pressurized and set aside for 12 hours.
8. Check the jars are sealed, label and store them in your pantry.

7. BEEF SHORT RIBS

Can beef short ribs to enjoy on their own as a starter or combined with vegetables or rice for a complete meal.

Prep time: 1 hour
Cook time: 1 hour 30 minutes
Makes: 1 quart

Ingredients

- 2 lbs beef short ribs
- Water/meat stock/tomato juice
- 1 tsp pickling salt

Method

1. Prepare the ribs so they will fit into the jars retaining the bones.
2. Heat a little fat or oil in a pan, brown the meat and leave to one side keeping it warm.
3. Prepare your jars and pack the meat into them leaving a 1- inch space at the top of each jar.
4. Add ½ tsp of salt to each jar.
5. Fill the jars leaving that 1-inch headroom with either boiling water, stock, or tomato juice.
6. Remove any air bubbles and top up if necessary.

7. Clean the rim of the jars and put on the lids and bands.
8. Process in your dial-gauge canner for 75 minutes at 11 lbs PSI at an altitude of 1-1,000ft and 75 minutes at 10 lbs PSI in a weighted-gauge canner. If you have used a quart jar keep the pressure the same but increase the processing time to 90 minutes.
9. Remove the jars from the canner once cooled and de-pressurized and leave to cool for 12 hours.
10. Check the jars are sealed, label and store them in your pantry.

Tip- when enjoying your beef short ribs please remember to remind your family of the bones.

8. STEAK WITH ONION GRAVY

A juicy meal packed full of flavor.

Process time: 75 minutes
Makes: 1 quart

Ingredients

- 1 pound eye of round steak
- 1 ½ cups beef broth
- 2 cups onions (chopped)
- 1 tbsp cooking oil
- ½ tsp salt

Method

1. Prepare your jars and add the specified amount of water to your pressure canner. Place the jars in your canner and heat on the stove until the water temperature is around 180 degrees F/82.2 degrees C.
2. In a pot add the broth and the salt and bring to a boil. Leave it simmering whilst you prepare the steaks.
3. Add oil to a pan and for 2-3 minutes sear each side of the steaks. Continue this until all the steaks have been seared, keeping them warm in a covered dish.
4. Return the broth to a boil whilst putting the steaks in the jars along with one cup of onions in each one-pint jar.
5. Transfer the broth into the jars leaving a 1-inch space at the top. Using

your bubble remover remove any bubbles and top up with more broth if necessary.

6. Clean the jar rims and add the lids and rings and place the jars into the canner. For 0-1,000 ft of altitude, you will need to process the jars for 75 minutes at 10 psi or 90 minutes if using a quart jar. The pressure will need to be altered if you live at a different altitude. Please refer to your specific canner's guidelines.

7. Once cooled and the pressure has been vented, take out the jars and set them to one side for 12 hours. Check that the seals are intact, label and put them in your pantry for up to a year.

8. When using, empty the liquid from the jars into a pot and heat until hot. Then add the steaks to the pot adding a teaspoon of flour to thicken the mixture. Turn down the heat to simmer for around 5 to 7 minutes. Can be served with rice or noodles.

9. CORNED BEEF AND POTATOES

A healthy quick meal for your family to share.

Prep time: 25 minutes
Cook time: 10 minutes Process time 75 minutes
Makes: 4 pints

Ingredients

- 4-5 lbs brisket
- 8- 10 cups potatoes
- Pickling spice blend (1/8 tsp per pint)
- Water

Method

1. Prepare your canner and warm the jars/lids/rings as per the canner's instructions.
2. Take off any fat from the brisket and cube.
3. Peel and cut the potatoes into cubes.
4. Add 1/8 tsp pickling spice to each jar. Boil the water and load the jars with the brisket and potatoes in layers leaving an inch of headspace. Add the boiling water continuing to leave the 1-inch headspace.

5. Remove any air bubbles and top up if necessary. Clean the rims of the jars and add the warmed lids and rings.
6. Process in your canner adhering to the specifications of your canner regarding the psi and adjusting for altitude.

10. SLOPPY JOE MIX WITH BEEF

Another great meal in a jar to have in your store, that's easy to prepare for your family to enjoy.

Prep time: 20 minutes
Cook time: 2 hours
Makes: 5 pints

Ingredients

- 1.5 lbs ground beef
- 1 cup tomato sauce
- ½ cup onion(diced)
- ½ cup beef broth
- ¼ cup bell pepper(diced)
- 1 ½ garlic cloves (crushed)
- 1/8 cup honey
- 1/8 cup apple cider vinegar
- ¾ tbsp Worcestershire sauce
- ¼ tbsp yellow mustard
- 1/8 tsp salt
- 1/8 tsp ground black pepper

Method

1. Prepare your canner and warm your jars.
2. In a pan brown the beef draining off any fat, and transfer to a pot.
3. Add the rest of the ingredients and bring up to a boil for 10 minutes.
4. Transfer the mixture to warm jars leaving 1-inch headspace. Remove any air bubbles and top up if necessary.
5. Clean the rims and place on the lids and ring. Transfer the jars to your canner and allow to boil, vent steam, and process for 1 hour 15 minutes at the pressure specified for your canner and altitude.

11. HAMBURGERS IN A JAR

A very handy store to have that's great for all the family, particularly the younger ones.

Prep time: 5 minutes
Cook time: 10 minutes
Canning time: 1 hour 30 minutes
Makes: 9 pints

Ingredients

- 7 ½ lbs ground beef
- Canning liquid (broth, tomato juice, or water)
- Seasoning (beef bouillon, taco mix, etc)
- Oil /beef fat (for browning)
- Salt and pepper to taste

Method

1. Prepare your canner and jar.
2. Season the meat and form it into equally sized patty shapes. Brown in a pan on both sides.
3. Pack the patties into the jars and cover them with boiling water, leaving 1-inch headspace.
4. Add the lids and rings and transfer the jars into your canner. Allow the canner to reach the required pressure depending on your model and the altitude.
5. Process for 75 minutes. Allow the canner to cool and lose its pressure. Then remove the jars and stand for 12-24 hours to cool.
6. Check the seals, remove the rings, label and store.

12. MEXICAN TACO MEAT

A meat mix full of flavor for those taco moments.

Prep time: 30 minutes
Cook time: 1 hour 30 minutes
Makes: 4 pints

Ingredients

- 2 lbs brisket beef (cut into chunks)
- Beef broth(hot)
- 2 cups onions (sliced)
- 2 chipotle chilies (in adobo sauce-finely chopped)
- 8 garlic cloves (sliced)
- ½ cup fresh coriander(chopped)
- 2 tsp oregano
- 2 tsp salt

Method

1. In a bowl add the salt, oregano, coriander, garlic, chilies, and onion. Combine well. Remove any fat from the meat and add it to the bowl.
2. Heat the broth.
3. Prepare your canner and warm the jars ready.
4. Mix the contents of the bowl well.
5. Fill the jars with the mixture leaving 1-inch headspace. Add the broth leaving the headspace still. Remove any air bubbles and top up, if necessary, with more broth.
6. Clean the rims of the jars, place the lids and rings on the jars, and process in your canner for 75 minutes.
7. Adjust the pressure according to your canner and the level of elevation.
8. Allow the canner to cool and lose pressure, remove jars and set aside to cool overnight.
9. Check seals, remove rings, label them, and store them in your pantry.

13. BEEF CURRY

Always a family favorite - a curry that is great to have as part of your store.

Process time: 75 minutes
Makes: 6 pints

Ingredients

- 2 ½ chuck roast (cubed)
- 2 large potatoes
- 5 oz plum tomatoes (peeled)
- 2 ½ onions (chopped)
- 2 serrano chilies
- Water
- 1 ¼ oz garlic
- 1 ¼ ox ginger
- 2 ½ tsp tomato puree
- 1 ¼ tsp chili powder
- 2 ½ tsp garam masala
- 2 ½ tsp tandoori masala
- 1 ¼ tsp turmeric
- 1 tsp salt
- 1/8 cup soy sauce
- Cilantro

Method

1. In a slow cooker add the onions and cook overnight.
2. Prepare your canner and 6-pint jars, lids, and rings.
3. In a pot add the tomatoes, chilies, ginger, and garlic and combine to form a paste.
4. Put the onions in a large pot, along with the beef, prepared paste, spices, and soy sauce, and brown the meat.
5. Fill the jars ¾ way to the top and finish off with the potatoes and cilantro. Ensure you leave a 1-inch headspace. Top up with water. Remove any air bubbles and top up if necessary. Add the lids and the rings.
6. Process in your canner for 75 minutes adhering to the correct pressure for your canner and your elevation.
7. Once your canner has cooled and the pressure has returned to normal the jars can be removed. Leave to cool overnight.
8. Check the seals, remove the rings, label and store.

14. CHIPOTLE MEATBALLS

A spicy dish for your family. Enjoy with tortillas or on a bed of rice.

Process time: 75 minutes
Makes: 5 pints

Ingredients Meatballs

- 2 lb ground beef
- 1 lb ground pork
- 1 cup onions (sliced)
- 6 tbsp potato flakes
- 3 tbsp coriander (minced)
- 1 ½ tsp dried oregano
- 1 tsp ground cumin
- Salt and pepper (to taste)

Method

1. Combine all the ingredients and form into balls of 1 ½ inch.
2. Brown them in a pan with oil and place them in an oven on low to keep warm.

Ingredients Sauce

- 6 garlic cloves (chopped)
- 1 large onion (diced)
- 1 tbsp vegetable oil
- 5 chipotles (stemmed and chopped in adobo sauce)
- 5 tbsp adobo sauce (from the chilies)
- 3 cups tomato sauce
- 2 cups beef broth

Method

1. Begin by frying the onions and garlic in the oil. Then add the rest of the sauce ingredients and bring to a boil. Reduce and simmer for 15 minutes or until the sauce thickens. Puree the sauce until nice and smooth.
2. Pour the sauce into the pan, add the meatballs and stir to warm them through.
3. Share the meatballs amongst the jars and top up with the sauce, leaving 1-inch headspace. Remove any air bubbles and top up if necessary.

4. Clean the jar rims and put on the lids and rings.
5. Process in the canner for 75 minutes at the pressure specific to your canner and altitude.
6. Leave the jars to cool overnight. Check the seals, remove the rings, label them, and store them (if you wait to eat them that is?).

15. SAUSAGE IN A JAR

Add vegetables and potatoes for a meal sure to be a hit with the whole family.

Prep time: 30 minutes
Cook time: 1 hour 30 minutes
Makes: 4 pints

Ingredients

- 3 lbs of sausage
- Water

Method

1. Cut the sausage meat into small balls.
2. Clean and prepare the jars, add 1 inch of water to your canner and place the jars inside over medium heat to preheat them.
3. In a frying pan brown the sausage meat, draining off any excess fat.
4. Transfer the cooked meat into the jars leaving an inch of headspace.
5. Add boiled, water, stock, or tomato juice maintaining the inch space at the top of the jars.
6. Remove any air bubbles, top up if any more fluid is required, clean the rims of the jars and attach the lids and rings.
7. Process in your prepared canner for 75 minutes at 10 lbs psi for a weighted-gauge canner at 0-1,000ft altitude and 75 minutes at 11 lbs psi for a dial-gauge canner at 0-1,000ft altitude.
8. Remove the jars once your canner has cooled and depressurized and set aside to cool for 12 hours.
9. Check the jars are sealed, label and store them in your pantry.

16. GROUND PORK

A great store for your pantry, useful for stir-fries, adding to various pasta sauces, or your casserole pot.

Prep time: 1 hour
Cook time: 1 hour 30 minutes
Makes: 6 pints

Ingredients

- 6 lbs ground pork
- Water
- Pinch of salt(optional)

Method

1. In a pan add a little oil or fat and brown the meat. Transfer it to a bowl with a lid to keep it warm until you have browned all the meat.
2. Prepare your jars and lids.
3. Fill the jars loosely with the browned meat, leaving 1-inch headspace, and add a pinch of salt to taste.
4. Fill the jars to within the 1-inch space with either boiling water, stock, or tomato juice.
5. Remove any air bubbles and top up if required, still leaving the 1-inch headspace.
6. Wipe the rims of the jars, put on the lids and rings and transfer the jars to your pressure cooker.
7. Process in your prepared pressure cooker for 75 minutes at 10 lbs psi for a weighted-gauge canner and 11 lbs psi for a dial-gauge canner for 0-1,000 ft of elevation. Adjust the pressure according to guidelines if you live at higher altitudes.
8. Remove the jars once the canner has cooled and depressurized and set aside to cool for 12 hours.
9. Check the jars are sealed, label and store them in your pantry.

17. PULLED PORK

A tasty meat to prepare to add to tacos or buns for a delicious lunch for your family.

Prep time: 20 minutes
Cook time: 1 -2 hours
Makes: 20 servings

Ingredients

- 5 lb of slow-cooked/barbecued pork.
- 1 pint BBQ sauce (optional)
- 1 quart of water or beef stock

Method

1. Add the recommended amount of water to your canner and clean your jars and lids and heat them in the canner bringing it to a simmer.
2. Bring to a gentle boil the beef stock or water in a pot.
3. Remove the jars from your canner and fill them ¾ full with the separated meat.
4. Either add 1/8 pint of the barbecue sauce to each jar or the prepared stock/water leaving the 1-inch headspace.
5. Remove any air bubbles and top up if necessary.
6. Wipe clean the rims of the jars and add the lids and rings to your jars.
7. Place the jars in your canner on the rack, put on the lid, and bring it to a boil.
8. After venting the steam for 10 minutes, close the vent by adding your weighted gauge or pressure regulator (dial-gauge canner). Process for 75 minutes at 10lbs of psi for weighted-gauge canner or 11lbs of psi for dial-gauge for 0-1,000ft of elevation.
9. Turn off the heat and allow it to cool and de-pressurize naturally. Then you can open the vent.
10. Remove the canner lid, wait for 10 minutes, then remove the jars after 10 minutes and leave to cool overnight.
11. Check the lids and seals, label and store them in your pantry.

18. PORK AND BEANS

A tasty accompaniment to other grilled or barbecued foods

Prep time: 30 minutes
Cook time: 1 hour 15 minutes
Makes: 4 pints

Ingredients

- 1 lb great northern beans/navy beans
- 4 pieces of salted pork
- 1 onion (chopped)
- 1 tbsp honey
- 1-pint tomato sauce
- 1 ½ cups of water
- 1/8 cup of brown sugar
- ½ tsp yellow mustard
- ¾ tsp to 1 ½ tbsp salt

Method

1. Soak the beans in a pot overnight covered with 3 inches of water.
2. Prepare your jars and lids and warm them before use in your canner.
3. Add the correct amount of water to your canner.
4. Rinse the beans and transfer them to a pot with water and bring to a boil for ½ hour.
5. In a pot add the sugar, mustard, tomato sauce, honey, and water, and bring to a boil until all the sugar has dissolved.
6. Add ¼ lb of beans to each jar, along with ¼ chopped onion, and divide the sauce equally among the jars. Add 1 piece of the salted pork to each jar.
7. Top up the jars with boiling water, leaving the 1-inch headspace. Remove any air bubbles and top up if necessary.
8. Clean the rims of your jars and attach the lids and rings.
9. Put the jars in your canner and seal the lid and put on high heat, allowing the canner to vent. Add your regulator /weight and bring your canner up to the required pressure and start your timer.
10. Process in your canner for 75 minutes, adjusting the psi according to your altitude.

11. Remove the jars from the canner once cooled and depressurized and set aside for 12 hours.
12. Check the jars are sealed, label and store them in your pantry.

19. PORK AND SQUASH STEW

A stew that's packed with vitamins and minerals, a healthy nutritious meal for your family.

Prep time: 25 minutes
Cook time: 30 minutes
Makes: 6 pints

Ingredients

- 1 ½ lb boneless pork shoulder(chopped)
- 4 dried red California chiles (remove stems)
- ¾ cup diced red onion
- 4 garlic cloves (crushed)
- 2 cups tomatoes (peeled and diced)
- 2 ½ cups acorn squash (peeled, seeded, and cut into chunks.
- 2 ½ cups butternut squash (peeled, seeded, and cut into chunks
- 1-quart chicken stock
- 1 cup water
- 2 cups boiling water
- 1 ½ tbsp olive oil
- ½ tbsp ground coriander
- ½ tsp sea salt
- ¼ tsp black pepper
- ½ tbsp oregano
- ¼ tsp red pepper flakes (crushed)

Method

1. To rehydrate the dried California Chile, submerge them in a bowl of boiling water for 15 minutes
2. Brown the pork in a pan (3-5 minutes) and leave to one side.
3. Strain the chilies reserving ½ cup of liquid. Place the chilies in a blender with the reserved liquid to make a paste and put it on one side.
4. Add the red pepper flakes, salt, pepper, oregano, onions, garlic, and cori-

ander to the pot the pork browned in and cook until the onions are clear (approx. 5-8 minutes)

5. Add the pork, squash, tomatoes, stock, and 1 cup of water. Bring to a boil for 5 minutes, finally adding the chili puree and mixing well. Reduce the heat to simmer for another 5 minutes.

6. Transfer the stew to the jars, leaving a 1-inch headspace. Remove any air bubbles and top up if necessary.

7. Clean the rims and place on the lids and rings. Transfer the jars to the canner and process for 75 minutes with the correct pressure for your canner and your altitude.

8. Allow the canner to cool and lose pressure naturally. Remove the jars and leave overnight to cool. Check the seals, remove the rings, label and store.

20. PORK ROAST

A delicious meal which can be served with vegetables and potatoes.

Prep time: 1 hour
Cook time: 1 hour 30 minutes
Makes: 7 pints

Ingredients

- 5 lbs pork shoulder (cubed)
- 7 cups of chicken broth
- 1 16 oz jar of pepperoncini (sliced) and brine
- 3 ½ tbsp of ranch seasoning mix. (Not containing buttermilk)
- ½ tbsp kosher salt
- ½ tsp ground black pepper

Method

1. Prepare your canner with the specified amount of water and clean your jars and lids. Heat an oven to 425 degrees F/218 degrees C.

2. Adding some salt and pepper to your pork lay the cubes on a baking sheet.

3. Roast them in the oven for 30 minutes (stir halfway through cooking)

4. In a pot add the chicken broth and bring to a boil, then cover and simmer for 10 minutes.

5. Divide the pork between the jars and add ½ tbsp of ranch mix, 1/8 to ¼ cup of pepperoncinis, and 1/8 cup of brine to each jar and top up to within the 1-inch headspace with the chicken broth.
6. Wipe clean the rims of the jars, add the lids and bands, and place them in your simmering canner.
7. Process the jars for 75 minutes and the correct psi for your altitude.
8. Remove the jars from your canner once it has cooled and depressurized and leave them to cool for 12 hours.
9. Check the seals, label them, and store them in your pantry.

21. MEXICAN PORK (RAW PACKED)

A flavorsome dish to have with rice, delicious for all the family to enjoy

Prep time: 15 minutes
Processing time: 1 ½ hours
Makes: 7 pints

Ingredients

- 10 lbs pork shoulder(cubed)
- ½ inch bay leaf
- ¼ tsp cumin
- ¼ tsp oregano
- 1/8 tsp garlic powder
- 1/8 tsp onion powder
- ¼ tsp concentrated orange juice
- ¼ tsp canning salt

Method

1. Prepare your pressure canner with the required water level and clean your jars and lids.
2. Prepare the pork by trimming off any excess fat and cutting it into cubes.
3. Divide the pork equally among the jars and add the spices, orange juice, seasoning, and bay leaf portion to each jar.
4. Place on hot lids and bands and transfer the jars to your canner and process for 75 minutes at 10lbs psi for an altitude of 0-1,000ft.
5. Leave your canner to cool naturally and depressurize and then remove your jars and set them aside to cool for 12 hours.

CANNING MEAT COOKBOOK FOR BEGINNERS

6. Check the jars are sealed, label and store them in your pantry.
7. When using, empty the contents of the jar into a pan to stir fry (removing the bay leaf) and accompany with your rice. Serve and enjoy.

22. SPARERIBS

Always a family favorite. Serve with salad or rice and beans for a delicious meal any time.

Prep time: 30 minutes
Processing time: 1 ½ hours
Makes: 4 pints

Ingredients

- Rack of pork (select good quality meat, cut into slices)
- Water
- Fat (to make the broth)
- Salt and pepper to taste

Method

1. Prepare your canner and clean the jars and lids.
2. Cut your meat into slices and trim off any gristle or fat.
3. Cook the meat in a pan until half done, remove the bones, cut it into squares, and season to taste. Transfer to a warm covered pot until ready to jar.
4. Add boiling water along with fat to the pan the meat cooked in at a ratio of 1 cup water to 2 tbsp fat and bring to a boil for 2-3 minutes to make the broth.
5. Add your jars to the canner on the rack and simmer at 180 degrees F/82 degrees C. Add the lids keeping the bands to one side.
6. Distribute the meat evenly amongst the jars and add the broth to each jar leaving the 1-inch headspace.
7. Remove the air bubbles and top up if necessary. Wipe the rims of the jars and add the lids and bands.
8. Place the jars in the canner, lock the lid, vent the steam for 10 minutes and then close the vent.
9. Once the canner has reached the correct pressure set the timer and process for 75 minutes. This is based on a weighted-gauge canner at

0-1,000ft of elevation. Adjust the pressure if using a dial-gauge pressure canner and if you are at a different elevation level.

10. Once completed turn off the heat and allow it to cool and lose its pressure. Wait 2 minutes, then remove the lid and the jars. Leave to cool for 24 hours. Check the jars are sealed before removing the bands. Clean the jar, label it, and store it in your pantry.

23. PORK AND APPLE CURRY

A tasty dish that can either be served as a stew or thickened and accompanied by rice.

Prep time: 40 minutes Process time: 75 minutes
Makes: 7 pints

Ingredients

- 3 ½ lbs pork shoulder(cubed)
- 2 large apples (peeled and chopped)
- 1 onion (chopped)
- 7 cups broth
- ¼ cup raisins
- 3 oz. orange juice
- 1 tbsp curry powder
- ½ tbsp garlic powder
- ¾ tbsp onion powder
- ½ tbsp ground ginger
- 1 tsp garam masala
- 2 tsp canning salt
- 1 ¼ tsp black pepper
- ½ tsp cinnamon

Method

1. Prepare your canner and jars, bringing your canner to a simmer.
2. Heat an oven to 425 degrees F/218 degrees C and place the pork on a tray and sprinkle 1 tsp salt and ¾ tsp pepper and roast for 30 minutes.
3. To make the broth in a pot add water, 1 tsp salt, ½ tsp pepper, raisins, onions, orange juice, and the rest of the seasonings into a pot, bring to a boil, cover, and reduce to a simmer for 10 minutes.

4. Add ½ lb of pork to each jar. Add the broth to the jars leaving 1-inch headspace. Remove any air bubbles and top up if necessary. Wipe the, add the lids and rings and transfer them to your canner.

5. Process for 75 minutes at the pressure required by your canner according to your altitude.

6. Allow to cool and lose pressure. Remove jars and allow to cool overnight. Check the seals, remove the rings, label and store.

24. SPICY SRIRACHA PORK

A dish packed full of flavor. Deliciously soft spiced pork. Serve with rice for a super tasty meal.

Prep time: 30 minutes
Cook time: 30 minutes
Makes: 7 pints

Ingredients

- 4 lbs pork shoulder(cubed)
- ½ onion
- 1 ½ large carrots
- 8 cups pork broth
- 7 garlic cloves (crushed)
- ¼ head cabbage(sliced)
- ½ cup soy sauce
- 1-2 tbsp sriracha sauce
- ½ tbsp ground ginger
- Salt and pepper to taste

Method

1. Prepare your canner and jars.
2. Heat an oven to 425 degrees F/218 degrees C. Season with salt and pepper, lay the meat on a tray, and roast for 30 minutes.
3. Turn on your canner to simmer and in a bowl mix the onions, carrots, and cabbage.
4. In a large pot add the ginger, soy sauce, and garlic and bring to a boil to make the broth. Reduce to simmer for 10 minutes.
5. In jars share equally the meat and the cabbage mixture until ¾ full. Then

add the broth to each jar leaving 1-inch headspace. Remove any air bubbles and top up if necessary.

6. Clean the rims, add the lids and rings and transfer not your canner.
7. Process for 75 minutes adjusting for canner type and pressure level depending on your altitude.

25. PORK MEATBALLS

A versatile storage jar to have to add to different recipes for making a variety of meals.

Prep time: 1 hour
Cook time: 1 hour 30 minutes
Makes: 10 servings

Ingredients

- 4 lbs Ground pork
- 4 tsp Mixed Herbs (e.g., oregano, parsley, marjoram, black pepper, onion powder, garlic powder, salt).
- Water (boiled)

Method

1. Prepare your canner and pint jars
2. Mix the pork and your choice of herbs and seasonings and form a meatball of around 3-4 inches in diameter.
3. Heat a small amount of oil in a pan and brown the meatballs.
4. Pack the meatball loosely in your jars leaving a 1- inch headspace.
5. Add boiling water to the jars maintaining the 1-inch headspace. Remove any air bubbles and top up if necessary.
6. Cleans the rims of the jars and put on lids and rings and process for 75 minutes adjusting for your canner's specifics and your altitude.
7. Remove from the canner and allow to cool overnight. Check seals, remove the rings, label and store.

26. SWEET AND SOUR PORK

A tasty dish for all to enjoy.

Process time: 75 minutes
Makes: 7 pints

Ingredients

- 2 ¼ lbs pork (remove fat and cube)
- 2 large carrots (peeled and sliced)
- 3 pints sweet and sour sauce (homemade if you have it)
- 1 green bell pepper (chopped)
- 1 red bell pepper (chopped)
- 1 onion (chopped)
- 1 can pineapple chunks (drained)
- Cooking oil

Method

1. Prepare your canner and jars.
2. Brown the pork in a frying pan with a little oil.
3. In a large bowl add the vegetables, pineapple, and meat. Add enough sauce to cover them and mix well.
4. Transfer the mixture to your jars leaving an inch of headspace. Remove any air bubbles and top up, if necessary, still leaving the inch headspace.
5. Clean the rims of the jars and add the lids and rings.
6. Transfer the jars to your canner and process for 75 minutes, adjusting the pressure for your canner and your altitude.
7. Remove jars when safe to do so and leave overnight to cool.
8. Check the seals, remove the rings, label them, and store them in your pantry.

CHAPTER 6
VENISON & RABBIT

27. VENISON STEW

A warming recipe packed full of vegetables.

Prep time: 30 minutes
Cook time: 2 hours
Makes: 7 pints

Ingredients

- 5-6 cups of beef broth
- 3 ½ cup venison stew meat (cubed)
- 2 cups potato (diced)
- 2 cups carrot (diced)
- 2 cups onion (chopped)
- 2 cups celery (chopped)
- 1/8 cup seasoning

Method

1. Prepare your canner with the correct amount of, water and clean your jars, rings, and lids.
2. In a pot bring the beef broth to a boil and reduce it to a simmer.
3. Season the meat with the seasoning mix and fill the jars with ¾ cup of meat and around ¼ cup of each of the vegetables.
4. Transfer the broth to the jars leaving an inch of headspace.
5. Clean the rims of the jars and add the lids and bands and transfer them to the rack in your pressure canner.
6. Process the jars in your canner for 75 minutes at 10 lbs psi for 0-1,000ft, adjusting the pressure if you live at a higher altitude.
7. Once completed turn off the heat, allowing for the canner to cool and

lose pressure. Remove weight (if using a weighted canner) and allow a further 10 minutes of cooling.

8. Remove the jars from your canner and set them to one side to cool for 12 hours.
9. Check the jars are sealed, label and store them in your pantry.

28. CANNED VENISON MEAT

Prepared meat that is ready to use in soups, stews, or sandwiches. Can also be accompanied by rice, potatoes, and vegetables to form a well-balanced meal.

Prep time: 15 minutes
Cook time: 1 hr 25 minutes
Makes: 8 servings

Ingredients

- 2 lb venison (cubed)
- 8 slices of onion
- 2 tbsp green bell pepper(minced-optional)
- 2 tsp garlic (crushed)
- 2 tsp salt
- 1/2 tsp ground black pepper

Method

1. Prepare your canner with the specified amount of water and clean your jars, lids, and rings.
2. Place the jars in your canner and simmer to warm the jars.
3. Mix in a bowl the venison, garlic, and seasoning.
4. Add the mix to the jars along with the bell pepper and onion. Wipe the rims of the jars and add the lids and rings.
5. Place the jars in your canner, cover them, and bring them up to a boil venting the pressure. Close the valve and observe the gauge until 10 psi is reached. Reduce the heat maintain the pressure and process for 75 minutes. When complete turn off the heat and allow the canner to cool and the pressure to return to zero.
6. Remove the jars and set them aside to cool for around 12 hours. Check the seals, label them, and store them in your pantry.

29. VENISON SPAGHETTI SAUCE

Prep time: 45 minutes
Cook time: 1 hour 10 minutes
Makes: 4 pints

Ingredients

- 1 ¼ lb ground venison
- ½ yellow onion(minced)
- 3 garlic cloves (crushed)
- ½ cup red wine
- 3 oz. tomato paste
- 1/8 cup fresh parsley(minced)
- 1 28 oz. can crushed tomatoes
- 1 tbsp dried oregano
- 1-pint venison stock
- ¼ tsp red pepper flakes
- 1/8 cup olive oil
- Salt and pepper to taste
- Sugar to taste

Method

1. Fry the venison in olive oil in a pot over medium heat. The amount of oil needed depends on the fatty content of the meat.
2. When browned add the onion and stir fry for 8 minutes. Add the garlic and cook for another 2 minutes, then add the tomato paste and cook for a further 2 minutes. Add the wine, red pepper flakes, and herbs and stir. Bring up to a boil, adding the stock and the crushed tomatoes.
3. Reduce to simmer for 30 minutes, seasoning to taste.
4. Meanwhile prep your canner and jars.
5. Transfer the sauce to the jars, leaving 1-inch headspace. Add the lids and rings and place them in the canner.
6. Process in your canner for 70 minutes once it's reached the correct pressure relating to your canner and your altitude.
7. Once processed remove the jars once the canner has cooled and lost pressure. Leave to cool overnight, check the seals, remove the rings, label, and store for up to 2 years.

30. VENISON SAUERBRATEN

A pot roast dish that's bursting with flavors.

Prep time: 10 minutes
Cook time: 2 hours
Makes: 10 servings

Ingredients

- 1/3 onion (chopped)
- 1/3 carrot (sliced)
- ¾ cup water
- 1/3 cup red wine vinegar
- 1/3 cup cider
- 1/3 tbsp kosher salt
- 1-2 lbs venison (cubed)

For the meat:

- ¼ tsp black pepper
- 1 bay leaf
- 2 whole cloves
- 4 juniper berries
- 1/3 tsp mustard seeds
- 1/6 cup sugar

To complete the recipe:

- 6 dark gingersnap biscuits (crushed)
- ¼ cup seedless raisins

Method

1. In a pan add the mustard seeds, cider vinegar, water, salt, pepper, bay leaf, cloves, juniper, red wine vinegar, and sugar, and bring to a boil. Then simmer for 10 minutes.
2. Into each pint jar add a layer of carrots and onions. Then add the raw venison until ¾ full, removing the bay leaf.
3. Add the hot marinade to the jars leaving 1-inch headspace. Remove any air bubbles and top up if necessary.
4. Clean the rims of the jars and add the lids and rings.

5. Place the jars in the canner and process for 75 minutes, adjusting the pressure for your canner and altitude.
6. To serve the dish add the jar's contents to a pot and simmer for 20 minutes.
7. Remove the meat and strain the liquid. Reheat the liquid, adding the gingersnaps. The mixture will thicken. Re-strain the liquid, adding the raisins. Serve the tender meat with the sauce.

31. VENISON CHILI

A chili made with venison for something a little different.

Prep time: 45 minutes
Cook time: 1 hour 20 minutes
Makes: 4 pints

Ingredients

*   3 lbs venison (any fat/tendons removed and chopped)
*   3 cups tomatoes (canned with juice)
*   1 cup onion (chopped)
*   ¼ cup chili powder
*   1 jalapeno pepper (seeded and minced)
*   1 garlic clove
*   2 ¼ tsp salt
*   ½ tsp cumin seed

Method

1. Prepare your canner and jars.
2. In a pan brown the venison meat (a lb at a time) and place it in a large pot. In the last batch add the onion and garlic and cook until they are clear.
3. Add all the remaining ingredients to the pot and bring to a boil. Reduce and gently boil for a further 20 minutes. Stir occasionally, removing any fat from the surface.
4. Transfer the mixture to the jars leaving an inch of headspace. Remove any air bubbles and top up if necessary. Clean the rims of the jars and add the lids and bands.

CANNING MEAT COOKBOOK FOR BEGINNERS

5. Transfer the jars to the canner and process for 75 minutes adjusting the pressure required for your canner and relative to your altitude.
6. Remove the jars when safe to do so and leave them to cool overnight.
7. Check the seals, remove the bands, label them, and store them in your pantry.

32. CANNED VENISON

Versatile meat that can be used in stews, sandwiches, etc

Prep time: 30 minutes
Cook time: 1 hour 15 minutes
Makes: 4 pints

Ingredients

- 4 beef bouillon cubes
- 3 ½ lbs raw deer meat
- 2 tsp canning salt
- 1 tbsp white vinegar

Method

1. In each jar add 1 beef bouillon cube, just over ¾ lb deer meat, ½ tsp salt, and ¼ tbsp white vinegar. Leave a 1-inch headspace.
2. Prepare your canner and warm the lids before putting them on the jars. and add the rings. Add the specified amount of water to your canner and place the jars inside. Process for 75 minutes at the required amount of pressure for your machine and altitude.
3. Allow the canner to cool and lose pressure. Remove jars and leave to cool overnight. Check seals, remove rings, label, and store in your pantry.

33. STEWED RABBIT

A healthy stew for the family to enjoy

Prep time 10 minutes
Cook time: 3 hours
Makes: 10 pints

Ingredients

- 1 large rabbit (cooked/bones removed)
- 3 lbs potatoes
- 1/5 celery stalk
- 1 lb. carrots
- ½ lb onions
- 2 ½ chicken bouillon cubes
- ¾ pint canned peas.

Method

1. In a pot put the rabbit and all the other ingredients and cook until the vegetables are soft.
2. Prepare your canner and jars. Transfer the mixture to your jars, clean the rims, add the lids and rings, and place in your canner.
3. Process for 75 minutes at the required pressure for your canner and your altitude.
4. Allow to cool and lose pressure before removing the jars. Remove them from the canner and leave them overnight to cool.
5. Check the seals, remove the rings, label them, and store them in your pantry.

34. RABBIT CASSEROLE

A versatile meal in a jar that can be used to make a casserole, rice or pasta dish, or a filling soup for your family.

Process time: 75 minutes
Makes: 8 pints

Ingredients

- 10 lbs rabbit meat (cubed)

- 1 tbsp parsley
- 1 tbsp salt
- ½ tsp pepper
- Water
- 2 cups carrots (peeled and sliced)
- 2 cups celery(chopped)
- 1 cup onion(sliced)

Method

1. Place the rabbit meat in a large pot with seasoning, cover it with water and bring it to a boil. Reduce to simmer until the meat begins to fall from the bones. Leave to cool down.
2. Prepare your canner and place the jars in the canner in simmering water.
3. Remove the meat from the bones and remove any excess fat. Keep the broth.
4. Add the vegetables to the broth and bring it back up to boiling. Return the meat to the pot and stir.
5. Remove just the meat and vegetables from the pot and transfer them equally to the warm jars leaving 1 inch of headspace. Then add the broth to the jars, maintaining the 1-inch headspace.
6. Cleans the rims of the jars, add the lids and rings and transfer them to the canner. Process for 75 minutes adjusting the pressure according to your canner and altitude.
7. When cooled and pressure lost remove the jars and set them aside to cool for 24 hours.
8. Check seals, remove rings, label and store.

35. RABBIT CACCIATORE

A tasty Italian comforting dish packed full of flavor.

Prep time: 10 minutes
Cook time: 1day 2 hours
Makes: 5 pints

Ingredients

- 9 portions of rabbit saddle /loin meat (cut into serving size)

- 1 medium onion (sliced)
- 2 pints tomatoes (diced)
- ¾ lbs mushrooms (sliced)
- 3 garlic cloves
- ¼ cup dried basil
- ½ cup chicken stock (warmed)

Method

1. Prepare the canner and warm the jars.
2. Brown the rabbit in a pan with olive oil.
3. Put the tomatoes, garlic, mushrooms, herbs, and onions in a pot and simmer for 15 minutes. Remove from the heat.
4. Put 2-3 pieces of the rabbit into each jar and then fill with the sauce, leaving an inch of headspace. Remove any air bubbles and top up if necessary, continuing to leave the inch headspace.
5. Clean the rims of the jars and add the lids and rings.
6. Transfer your jars to the rack on the bottom of your canner. Process for 75 minutes at the recommended pressure for your canner and based on your altitude.
7. Allow the canner to cool and pressure to return to zero. When safe remove the jars and leave them to cool overnight.
8. Check seals, remove the rings, label them, and store them in your pantry.

CHAPTER 7
CHICKEN & TURKEY

36. CANNED CHICKEN

Having a supply of prepared chicken in your pantry will come in handy for making lots of different meals for your family. Here's how to pressure can your chicken.

Prep time: 1 hour
Cook time: 1 hour
Canning time: 1 hour 30 minutes
Makes: 4 servings

Ingredients

- 1 whole Chicken
- Chicken broth
- Salt
- Oil

Method

1. If using a whole chicken, then separate it into the pieces you wish to can. The carcass of the chicken can be used to make the broth. You can also use prepared chicken from the store and prepared chicken broth. Chicken can be canned with or without bones, skinned or skinless, and in different sizes.
2. Prepare and heat your pressure canner and clean your jars, lids, and rings.
3. In a pan with oil brown the chicken and transfer to your jars leaving a 1 ¼ inch headspace. Add a little salt if you wish. ½ tsp per pint.
4. Pour the chicken broth into the jars maintaining the space, remove any air bubbles and top up if necessary.
5. Clean the rims of the jars and place them on the lids and rings.
6. Place the jars in your canner, put on the lid and turn on the heat and

vent the steam for 10 minutes. Then seal the canner and bring it up to the required pressure depending on your canner and the altitude. Begin the timer and process for 75 minutes for pint jars/ 90 minutes for quarts for boneless chicken and 65 minutes for pint jars/75 minutes for quarts for boned chicken.

7. Once processed turn off the heat and allow the canner to cool and lose its pressure. Then remove the jars and allow them to cool.
8. Check the jars have been sealed properly, remove the bands, label them, and store them in your pantry for 12 to 18 months.

37. CHICKEN AND GRAVY

Add rice or potatoes to complete this tasty family meal.

Prep time: 30 minutes
Cook time: 1 hour 30 minutes
Makes: 4 pints

Ingredients

- 2 lb boneless chicken
- 1 cup potato (cubed)
- 1 cup celery (chopped)
- 1 cup onion (chopped)
- Chicken stock/water
- 2 tsp poultry seasoning
- 4 tbsp dry white wine
- 1 tsp ground black pepper
- 2 tsp salt

Method

1. Prepare your canner and clean the jars, lids, and rings and warm the jars in the canner in the specified amount of water.
2. Cut the chicken into cubes and place it in a bowl with the onion, celery, and potato. Then mix in the rest of the other ingredients apart from the broth.
3. Prepare the chicken stock and set it aside.
4. Pack the warm jars with the mixture leaving the 1-inch headspace and

then add the stock, remove any air bubbles and top up, if necessary, still leaving the 1-inch headspace.

5. Wipe the rims of the jars, place them on the lids and rings, and process them according to your specific canner. For weighted gauge 75 minutes at 10lbs psi and 75 minutes at 11 lbs of psi for dial-gauge (based on an altitude of 0-1,000ft)

6. Allow the canner to cool and depressurize before removing the jars. Allow to cool for 12 hours, remove the rings, label, and store in your pantry.

7. When using, heat through properly the contents of the jars and stir in some flour to thicken the gravy. Delicious!

38. CHICKEN PIE FILLING

This a tasty recipe to have prepared when making a chicken pie for your family to enjoy. Once prepared just make your pie crust to top this yummy filling.

Process time: 75 minutes
Makes: 7 pints

Ingredients

- 5 chicken breasts (chopped)
- 2 cups frozen peas
- 2 ½ cups chopped carrots
- 1 cup celery (chopped)
- 1 cup onions (chopped)
- 4 cups chicken broth
- 4 pints water
- 2 tbsp butter
- ½ tbsp salt
- 1 tsp black pepper
- 1 tsp garlic powder
- 1 tsp celery seeds
- ½ cup canning gel

Method

1. Prepare your canner and clean the jars, lids, and bands and warm the jars in your canner.

2. Boil the chicken in a pot until cooked, remove, allow to cool, and chop into pieces. Keep the liquid in the pot.

3. In a pot add the celery, butter, and onions and cook on medium heat until the onions are clear. Add the broth, salt, pepper, peas, carrots, and chicken, and bring it up to a boil.

4. In a bowl add 1 ½ cups of the liquid from the chicken pot and mix in the canning gel. Add this to the stock pot and thoroughly mix. Bring up to a boil for 5 minutes. Add more chicken water if the mixture is too thick. Remove from heat.

5. Fill the jars leaving the inch headspace with the pie filling mixture. clean the rims, add the lids and bands and return to your canner.

6. Process the jars at 10 psi for 75 minutes adjusting according to your level of elevation/canner type.

7. Allow your canner to cool and lose pressure before removing jars. Leave jars to cool for 12 hours, check seals, remove the bands, label, and store.

39. CHILI CHICKEN AND BEANS

A healthy and delicious chili for the family to enjoy. Serve with your favorite rice.

Prep time: 12 hours
Cook time: 45 minutes Pressure can time: 1 hour 30 minutes
Makes: 6 servings (3 pint jars)

Ingredients

- 1 ½ cups boneless chicken(cubed)
- ¼ onion(chopped)
- ¾ cup great northern beans (leave to soak overnight before use)
- 2 garlic cloves (crushed)
- ¼ tbsp olive oil
- 2 ½ cups chicken broth
- ¼ cup green chilies (diced)
- 1/8 cup ground cumin
- ¼ tbsp oregano(dried)
- ¼ tsp cayenne pepper

Method

1. Prepare your canner, jars, lids, and bands, and warm the jars before use in your canner during the final 10 minutes of simmering. (no.6)
2. Add the beans in their liquid to a pot and simmer for 30 minutes.
3. Put another large pot on medium heat and add the oil. Add the chicken to the pot and cook for 10 minutes.
4. Add the herbs and spices, garlic, and onions, and cook for another 5 minutes.
5. Drain the water from the beans and add them to the chicken pot.
6. Finally add the chilies and the broth, bring them up to a boil, then simmer for 10 minutes.
7. Divide the mixture between the 3 jars, leaving the 1-inch headspace.
8. Remove bubbles, top up, clean the jar rims and add the lids and bands.
9. Process in your canner for 75 minutes with the pressure recommended by your manufacturer according to altitude and type of canner used.
10. Remove jars after processing, leave to cool for 12 hours, check the seals, remove the bands, label, and store in your pantry.

40. GREEN CHILI CHICKEN

With the addition of rice, this recipe makes for a meal packed full of flavor for your family to enjoy.

Prep time: 30 minutes
Cook time: 1 hour 30 minutes
Makes: 4 pints

Ingredients

- 2 lb boneless chicken breast(cubed)
- 1 cup white kidney beans (cooked and drained)
- 1 cup green onion(chopped)
- 1 cup roasted salsa verde
- 2 clove garlic
- Chicken stock (hot)
- 4 tbsp sliced pickled jalapenos (drained)
- 4 tbsp fresh coriander(chopped)
- 2 tsp salt

Method

1. Prepare your canner, jars, lids, and bands, and warm the jars before use.
2. Place the chicken in a bowl, along with all the ingredients apart from the stock, and mix well.
3. Boil water to make your chicken broth when using cubes etc.
4. Pack the jars with the mixture leaving 1-inch headspace. Top up with the broth, remove the bubbles and add more if necessary, keeping the headspace.
5. Clean the rims of the jars, put on the lids and bands, and process in your canner for 75 minutes at 10 psi for weighted gauge and 11 lbs psi for dial-gauge for an altitude of 0-1,000ft. Adjust pressure if you live at higher altitudes.
6. Remove jars after cooling/de-pressurizing and set aside for 12 hours.
7. Check seals, and remove bands, label, and shelf for future use.

41. SWEET AND SOUR CHICKEN

A tasty recipe enjoyed by all the family. Serve with rice for this classic dish.

Prep time: 10 minutes
Cook time: 2 hours 20 minutes
Makes: 5 pints

Ingredients

- 2 ¼ lbs boned skinless chicken(cubed)
- 1 large green pepper(chopped)
- ½ large red pepper(chopped)
- 1 onion(chopped)
- 1 ½ can pineapple chunks (drained/keep the sauce)
- ¼ cup brown sugar
- ¾ cup white vinegar
- 3 tbsp soy sauce
- 2 tbsp ketchup
- ½ tsp powdered ginger

Method

1. Prepare your canner and 5 pint jars.
2. In a pot add the pineapple juice, brown sugar, vinegar, soy sauce, ketch-

up, ginger, and ¼ cup water and bring gently to a boil, dissolving the sugar.
3. In the jars layer the chicken, pineapple, onions, and peppers and then pour the liquid in leaving 1-inch headspace.
4. Process the jars for 75 minutes at 10 lbs psi for weighted-gauge and 11 lbs psi for dial-gauge canners. Adjust the pressure if you live at a higher altitude.

42. GREEK CHICKEN

A dish packed full of flavor

Prep time: 15 minutes Process time: 75 minutes
Makes: 7 pints

Ingredients

- 7 lbs chicken breast (cut into chunks)
- 14 garlic cloves (crushed)
- 7 tbsp lemon juice
- 7 tsp lemon pepper
- 7 tsp Dijon mustard
- 3 ½ tsp oregano(dried)
- 1 ¾ tsp sea salt
- Filtered water (to top up jars)

Method

1. Prepare your canner, adding the specified amount of water. Wash the jars, lids, and rings ready for your recipe.
2. Load each jar to within 1 ½ inch from the top with the chicken chunks. Then add 2 garlic cloves, 1 tbsp lemon juice, ¼ tsp salt, 1 tsp lemon pepper, ½ tsp oregano, and 1 tsp Dijon mustard to each jar. Stir all the contents and remove any air bubbles. Then add the filtered water to each jar leaving a 1 ¼ inch headspace.
3. Clean the rims of the jars and place on the lids and rings.
4. Place the jars in the canner and process for 75 minutes, using the pressure for your altitude.

43. CHICKEN MARSALA

Served with rice, this dish is sure to be a tasty treat for your family

Prep time: 10 minutes
Cook time: 1 day 3 hours
Makes: 5 pints

Ingredients

- 2 ½ -3 ½ lbs boneless chicken (cut into cubes)
- 2 ½ cups mushrooms (sliced)
- 1-quart chicken stock
- 1 cup dry Marsala wine
- ½ onion(chopped)
- 1/ 2 tsp garlic(chopped)
- ½ tsp oregano
- Salt
- Pepper

Method

1. In a pan fry the chicken with salt and pepper to taste. Set aside and keep warm.
2. Prepare your canner and jars. Load the jars with 1 cup of chicken, along with ½ cup of mushrooms. In the frying pan add the onion, garlic, and oregano. Fry until soft, then add the wine and bring to a boil. Then add the chicken stock.
3. Bring back to boil, then reduce to simmer for 2-3 minutes.
4. Fill the jars with the stock mixture leaving 1-inch headspace, remove any air bubbles and top up if necessary.
5. Clean the rims, add the lids and rings and place your jars on the rack in your canner.
6. Process for 75 minutes at the required pressure for your canner depending on your altitude. Leave jars to cool overnight.
7. When using this mix, heat the contents of the jar in a pan and thicken the liquid with some flour, add some cream/sour cream and serve with rice. Delicious!

44. FAR EASTERN CHICKEN

A tasty Asian dish in a jar to enjoy with rice and crackers.

Prep time: 30 minutes
Cook time: 15 minutes
Makes: 7 pints

Ingredients

- 4 ½ lbs chicken (cubed)
- 2 ½ carrots (diced)
- 1 onion(chopped)
- 7 garlic cloves
- 6 cups chicken broth
- ¼ cup soy sauce
- ½ tbsp onion powder
- ½ tbsp ground ginger
- ¾ tsp garlic powder
- 1/8-1/4 tsp cayenne pepper

Method

1. Prepare your canner. Add water and bring the canner up to a simmer. Wash and prepare the jars, lids, and rings.
2. In a pot add the broth, soy sauce, ginger, garlic, and onion powder and bring to a boil. Then cover and reduce to simmer for 10 minutes.
3. Divide the carrots, onions, and chicken evenly amongst the jars. Add a clove of garlic to each one and fill with the broth, leaving an inch of headspace. Remove any air bubbles and top up if necessary. Wipe the rims and add the lids and rings.
4. Process in your canner for 75 minutes at the required psi for your canner and altitude.

45. BUTTER CHICKEN

A familiar dish that all the family will enjoy with various sides.

Prep time: 30 minutes Process time: 75 minutes
Makes: 8 servings

Ingredients

- 1 ½ cups tomatoes (crushed)
- 1 cup onion (diced)
- 1 tbsp olive oil
- 1 tbsp paprika
- 1 tbsp curry powder
- ¾ tbsp coriander leaves
- ¾ lb chicken breast (cubed)
- 2 tsp garlic (minced)
- 1 tsp green chilies (diced)
- 1 tsp kosher salt
- 1 tsp ginger (minced)

Method

1. Prepare the canner and warm the jars in the canner (bring to a boil).
2. In a pan fry the garlic, onion, and ginger until brown. Leave to drain on a paper towel.
3. Warm the lids of the jars in the canner.
4. Return the onion mix to a pot, adding the tomatoes and the spices. Bring to a boil, adding extra chili if you like it hot.
5. Add the chicken and return to boil. Then remove from the heat.
6. Transfer the contents of the pot into the warm jars leaving 1-inch headspace. Remove any air bubbles, top up, if necessary, clean the rims and add the lids and rings.
7. Process in the canner for 75 minutes at the pressure required by your canner and depending on your altitude.
8. The jars can then be removed and left to cool overnight.
9. Then check the seals, remove the rings, label and store.
10. When serving, merely heat for 5 minutes and serve with rice, pasta, potatoes, or naan bread. Delicious!

46. BOURBON CHICKEN

A dish full of flavor, super delicious served with rice.

Process time: 75 minutes
Makes: 6 pints

Ingredients

- 4 lbs chicken (cubed)
- ½ cup apple juice
- 2/3 cup light brown sugar
- 1 cup water
- 2/3 cup soy sauce
- 4 tbsp oil
- 4 tbsp tomato ketchup
- 2 tbsp cider vinegar
- 2 garlic cloves (crushed)
- 2 tsp red pepper(crushed)

Method

1. Add all the ingredients (apart from the chicken and the oil) to a pan and bring to a boil.
2. Prepare your canner and jars.
3. Share the chicken equally amongst the jars, then top up with the sauce from the pan, leaving an inch of headspace in each jar. Add the lids and the rings.
4. Place the jars in the canner and process for 75 minutes at the pressure required by your canner and adjusting for your altitude.
5. Remove the jars once the canner has cooled and lost the pressure and leave for 24 hours to cool.
6. Check seals and remove the rings. Label and store.

47. ROSEMARY CHICKEN

Something different for your store with this simple chicken dish with a sophisticated taste.

Prep time: 10 minutes
Cook time: 1 hour 15 minutes
Makes: 5 pints

Ingredients

- 5 lbs boneless chicken (cut into chunks)
- 10 2-inch rosemary sprigs
- 5 tsp salt

Method

1. Prepare your canner and your jars. Place a sprig of rosemary in each jar and fill with chicken up to 1 ½ inch from the top. Add another rosemary sprig and the tsp of salt.
2. Clean the rims of the jars and place on the lid and bands.
3. Process in your canner for 75 minutes at the correct psi for your elevation and canner.
4. Leave the jars to cool overnight once removed from the canner. Check the seals, remove the bands, label them, and store them in your pantry to enjoy on that special occasion.

48. CANNED TURKEY

Handy meat to use in many dishes for your family to enjoy.

Prep time: 45 minutes
Cook time: 3 hours 20 minutes
Makes: 8 servings

Ingredients

- 9 lb turkey
- 2 quarts turkey stock (hot)
- Canning salt

Method

1. Preheat oven to 350 degrees F/176.7 degrees C. Place the bird breast side up on a roasting tin with a rack on the base. Remove the neck and giblets and put these under the turkey.
2. Roast the chicken until cooked. check the internal temperature of the bird which should be 165 degrees F/73.9 degrees C. Once cooked take the meat from the bones and cut it into chunks.
3. Prepare your canner and jars. Place the jars in the canner on the rack and half fill them with water and bring the canner to a simmer at 180 degrees F/82.2 degrees C to warm them before use.
4. Add the stock to a pot and bring it to a boil, then reduce to simmer to keep warm.
5. One at a time remove a jar empty the water and fill it with the turkey, leaving 1-inch headspace. Add ½ tsp salt and pour in the stock maintaining the 1-inch headroom. Remove any air bubbles and top up if necessary. Clean the rims of the jars and add the lids and bands.
6. Process for 75 minutes at 10 lbs psi for weighted-gauge and 11 lbs psi for dial-gauge canners. Adjust the psi if at a different altitude to 0-1,000ft.
7. Once the canner has cooled and lost its pressure, wait for 10 minutes, then remove the jars and leave them to cool for 12-24 hours.
8. Check the seals, remove the rings, label them, and store them in a cool place and use them within a year.

49. ORIENTAL TURKEY MEATBALLS

A healthy meatball full of flavors of the east.

Prep time: 10 minutes
Cook time: 2 hours 30 minutes
Makes: 10 servings

Ingredients

- 1 ½ lb of ground turkey
- 2 ½ green onions (chopped)
- 1 inch piece of ginger(grated)
- 2 ½ garlic cloves (grated)
- ½ tsp garlic powder
- 2 ½ tbsp teriyaki ginger sauce

- Chicken stock
- 1 tbsp soy sauce
- 1 ½ tsp salt
- ½ tsp ground pepper
- Red pepper flakes

Method

1. Add the ingredients to a bowl, mix well and form the mixture into similar-sized meatballs. Transfer the balls onto a non-stick tray and bake in an oven for 45 minutes at 350 degrees F/176.7 degrees C.
2. Load the balls into the jars and add hot chicken stock, leaving a 1-inch headspace. Remove any air bubbles, clean the rims of the jars, and place on the lids and rings.
3. Process in your canner for 75 minutes at 10 lbs psi for weighted-gauge and 11 lbs psi for dial-gauge. You should make around 30 meatballs.

50. POZOLE VERDE TURKEY

A classic Mexican dish to use up that Thanksgiving turkey.

Prep time: 1 hour 30 minutes
Cook time: 15 minutes Pressure canning process:1 hour 15 minutes
Makes: 6 pints

Ingredients

- 1 ½ cups turkey(chopped)
- 6 cups turkey broth
- 7 tomatillos (chopped)
- 1 ½ 15 oz. cans hominy(drained)
- 1/2 cup cilantro(chopped)
- ¾ cup onions (chopped)
- 2 jalapenos (seeded and chopped)
- 1 poblano pepper (seeded and chopped)
- ¼ cup orange juice
- 1 ½ tbsp honey
- ½ tbsp ground cumin
- ½ tbsp dried oregano

Method

1. Place all the ingredients in a pot and bring to a boil for 5 minutes.
2. Prepare your canner and jars. Warm the jars.
3. Transfer, sharing equally the turkey and vegetables between the jars, then add the broth to each leaving 1-inch headspace. Clean the rims, add the lids and rings, and process in your canner for 75 minutes. Adjust the pressure according to your canner and level of altitude.
4. Allow the canner to cool and lose the pressure before removing the jars and allowing them to cool for 24 hours.
5. Check the seals, remove the rings, label and store.
6. To serve heat the contents of the jar in a pan, bring it up to a boil for 10 minutes, and serve with avocado, tortilla chips, or cheese. Delicious!

51. TURKEY AND GRAVY

A warming meal for your family to enjoy around the table.

Process time: 75 minutes
Makes: 4 pints

Ingredients

- 2 lbs turkey (cut in chunks)
- 1 cup onion(chopped)
- 1 cup celery(chopped)
- 1 ½ cups potatoes (peeled and cubed)
- 1-quart turkey broth
- 4 tsp salt
- 2 tsp black pepper
- 4 tsp poultry seasoning (contains- 1 tbsp each of rosemary, oregano, marjoram, thyme, and ½ tsp each of ginger and black pepper.
- 4 tbsp white wine (dry)

Method

1. Between the jars divide evenly the turkey, celery, onion, and potatoes last, up to the 1-inch headspace. Then add 1 tsp salt, ½ tsp pepper, 1 tsp poultry seasoning, and 1 tbsp white wine to each jar.
2. Then add the broth up to the 1-inch headspace. Remove any air bubbles and top up if necessary.

3. Place the jars in your canner and process for 75 minutes. Always adjust the pressure needed for your canner type and your altitude.
4. Allow the canner to cool and release the pressure and remove jars for cooling for 12-24 hours.
5. Check seals, remove rings, label and store.
6. When you use the jar's contents for your meal add a tbsp of flour to the liquid in the jar to thicken it when heating. Then add the rest of the contents and simmer for 10 minutes and enjoy.

52. TURKEY GOULASH

A traditional and full-flavored dish.

Process time: 75 minutes
Makes: 4 pints

Ingredients

- 2-3 lb of lean turkey
- 3 cups of tomato sauce
- 1 large onion (chopped)
- 1 cup hot or bell peppers (chopped)
- 6 cloves garlic (crushed)
- 3 tbsp Worcestershire sauce
- 2 tsp dry mustard
- 1 tsp red pepper flakes
- 1 tsp thyme
- 1 tsp cumin
- 1 tsp chipotle seasoning

Method

1. Prepare your canner and place your cleaned jars in the canner to warm.
2. In a pan brown the turkey with the onion and peppers. Add the garlic, season to taste, then drain.
3. In a large saucepan combine the meat mixture with the tomatoes, Worcestershire sauce, and the seasonings and simmer for around 30 minutes.
4. Transfer the mixture into the warm jars leaving 1-inch headspace. Remove any air bubbles and top up if necessary. Wipe the rims, add the

lid and rings and place them in the canner, and process for 75 minutes, adjusting for the level of elevation.

5. Leave the jars overnight to cool. Check seals, remove rings, label, and store in your pantry.

6. To serve, heat the goulash in a pan, bringing it to a simmer and adding (if required) any further spices or a little brown sugar to sweeten. Serve with pasta of your choice and enjoy!

CHAPTER 8
SOUPS, STOCKS AND BROTHS

53. CHICKEN & ASPARAGUS SOUP

A deliciously nutritious soup, full of goodness.

Prep time: 10 minutes
Cook time: 1 day + 1 hour
Makes: 10 servings

Ingredients

- ¾ lb asparagus (fresh, cut into ½ inch pieces)
- 2 cups chicken broth/stock
- ¼ cup shallots (minced)
- ¼ tbsp garlic(minced)
- Pinch salt
- Pinch white pepper
- 2 tsp Olive oil

Method

1. Prepare your canner, prep your jars, and warm in the canner until ready for use.
2. In a pan with oil fry the shallots and garlic until clear and heat the broth/stock in a pot. Remove from heat and set aside.
3. ¾ fill each jar with the asparagus. Top up with equal portions of shallots/garlic and season. Fill with the stock leaving a 1-inch headspace. De-bubble and top up if necessary.
4. Wipe the rims of the jars and add the lids and rings.
5. Place jars in your canner and process according to guidelines.
6. Process for 75 minutes at 10lbs psi (weighted-gauge) and 11lbs psi (dial-gauge). Adjust the psi according to altitude.
7. Once processed, remove jars and set aside for 12 hours to cool.

8. Check seals, remove rings, and label them before storage.
9. When serving, heavy cream and parmesan cheese can be added to the heated-up soup to make it extra creamy.

54. CARROT AND CELERY SOUP WITH CHICKEN STOCK

A creamy healthy soup for your family to enjoy.

Prep time: 25 minutes
Cook time: 1 hour 20 minutes
Makes: 6 pints

Ingredients

- 2 lbs carrots (peeled/sliced)
- ½ lb celery
- 6 cups chicken stock
- 1 ½ tbsp lemon juice
- 1 tbsp salt
- ½ tbsp olive oil
- 1 tsp onion powder
- ½ tsp ground black pepper
- ½ tsp coriander
- ½ tsp ginger
- ½ tsp thyme
- ¼ tsp cumin

Method

1. In a pot heat the oil and fry the celery. Add the carrots and 2 cups of stock. Simmer until the carrots are soft (around 30 minutes).
2. Allow the mixture to cool, puree, then return to the pot and add the remaining 4 cups of stock.
3. Bring to a boil, then simmer for 20-30 minutes. Add the various seasonings and spices according to your taste.
4. Transfer to warm jars previously prepared in your canner.
5. Leave a 1 -inch headspace, clean the rims, add the lids, and pressure cook.
6. Process for 40 minutes at 10 lbs psi for weighted gauge and 11 lbs psi

for dial-gauge canner based on 0-1,000ft of altitude. Adjust pressure according to your altitude.

7. Allow to cool and lose pressure, remove and leave to cool before checking the seals, labelling, and storing.

55. VEGETABLE & BEEF SOUP

A soup packed full of veg full of goodness for your family.

Prep time: 20 minutes
Cook time: 1day 2 hours
Makes: 6 pints

Ingredients

- 1 1/2 pounds cubed stewing beef
- 4 cups beef broth
- 1 cup chopped onion
- 3 carrots peeled and cubed
- 1 cup chopped celery
- 2 larges cubed potatoes
- 28 oz chopped canned tomatoes
- 1 tablespoon sugar
- 2 tsp salt
- ½ tsp black pepper
- 2tsp mixed herbs – rosemary, thyme, marjoram, basil

Method

1. Prepare 6-pint jars and keep them warm in your canner.
2. In a large pot, brown the meat then add all the ingredients, bring to a boil, reduce the heat and continue boiling for 10 minutes.
3. Use a slotted ladle first to fill the jars halfway with the meat and vegetables.
4. Fill the jars with the soup leaving the 1-inch headspace. Remove any air bubbles and top up if necessary.
5. Clean the rims of the jars, place on the lids and rings and transfer the jars to the rack in your canner and bring to a boil.
6. Process your jars for 75 minutes, adjusting the psi for your altitude. Turn off the heat and allow it to cool and lose pressure.

7. Remove the canner lid, wait 10 minutes, then remove the jars and leave to cool overnight.
8. Check the seals, remove the rings, label and store.

56. MUSHROOM & BEEF BROTH

A tasty soup on its own or a base for other dishes for your family to enjoy.

Prep time: 10 minutes
Cook time: 1 day 2 hours 30 minutes yields: 5 pints

Ingredients

- 2 ½ lbs mushrooms (sliced)
- 8 cups beef broth
- 6 cloves garlic(minced)
- 1 ½ tsp dried thyme
- ¼ tsp nutmeg

Method

1. Prepare your canner and jars and warm them in your canner whilst you prepare the recipe.
2. In a pot heat the broth, then remove to one side.
3. Fill the jars ¾ full of mushrooms and add 1 tsp of garlic, ¼ tsp dried thyme, and a pinch of nutmeg. Then add the hot broth leaving the 1-inch headspace. Remove the air bubbles and top up if necessary.
4. Clean the rims of the jars and put on the lids and rims.
5. Place the jars on the rack in your canner. Bring the canner to a boil.
6. Process for 75 minutes at 10 psi for weighted gauge and 11 psi for dial-gauge. Adjust for different altitudes.
7. After cooling, de-pressurizing, remove the jars, and leave to cool overnight.
8. Check seals, remove rings, and label before storing.
9. When using the soup, you can add a tbsp of butter and 1/8 cup of flour when heating it to make it creamier.

57. LEEK, CHICKEN & POTATO SOUP

A tasty and satisfying soup for those hungry moments

Prep time: 10 minutes
Cook time: 2 hours
Makes: 12 servings

Ingredients

- 5 lbs leeks (washed, soaked, and sliced)
- 6 medium-sized white potatoes
- 5-6 cups chicken stock

Method

1. Prepare your canner, allowing it to vent steam for it to reach the correct temperature and pressure necessary to process the food. Prepare your jars, lids, and rings.
2. Peel your potatoes and cut them into chunks and soak them in cold water. This will maintain their color.
3. Prepare the chicken stock by bringing it to a boil in a pan.
4. Add the leeks and potatoes to the jars and top up with the stock leaving 1-inch headspace.
5. Place the jars in your canner and process for 60 minutes at 10 lbs psi for the weighted-gauge canner and 11 lbs psi for the dial-gauge canner. Adjust psi if at higher altitudes than 0-1,000ft.
6. Remove jars from the canner when ready and leave to cool for 12 hours. Check seals, remove rings, label, and place in your pantry.

58. SPLIT PEA & HAM SOUP

A meal in a jar fit to satisfy those hungry appetites.

Prep time: 1 hour 30 minutes
Cook time: 1 hour 30 minutes
Makes: 5 pints

Ingredients

- 1 lb dry split peas
- 2 quarts broth or water

- 1 cup cooked ham(diced)
- 1 ½ cups carrots (sliced)
- 1 cup onion(chopped)
- 1 bay leaf
- ¼ tsp allspice
- Salt and pepper

Method

1. In a pot add 2 quarts of broth along with the peas and bring to a boil. Reduce to simmer until peas are cooked (1 hour approx.)
2. Puree the mixture for a smooth soup and return to the pot.
3. Add the onions and carrots to the pot along with the spices.
4. Prepare your canner and heat the jars ready in your canner.
5. Allow the soup to simmer for 30 minutes or until the vegetables are cooked and add more water if becoming too thick.
6. Remove the bay leaf and season to taste.
7. Fill the jars leaving a 1-inch headspace. Add the lids and rings and place them in your canner. Process for 75 minutes at 10lbs psi for weighted gauge and 11lbs for dial gauge at 0-1,000ft elevation.
8. Allow to cool and lose pressure. Remove the jars and set aside to cool overnight. Check seals, remove the rings, label and store.

59. BLACK BEAN & BEEF SOUP

A delicious dense soup full of nutritional goodness.

Prep time: 8 hours
Cook time: 1 hour 30 minutes
Makes: 4 pints

Ingredients

- ½ lb black beans (pre-soaked overnight)
- 2 ½ cups tomato puree
- 2 cups beef broth
- ¼ lb onions (chopped)
- 1/8 cup red wine vinegar
- 2 ½ garlic cloves
- 1 cup carrots (sliced)

- 2 bay leaves
- 2 tsp ground cumin
- 1 tsp oregano
- ½ tsp salt
- ½ tsp black pepper

Method

1. Drain the beans and add them to a pot along with 2 inches of water. Bring the water up to boil, then simmer for 30 minutes.
2. Drain the beans and return to the pot adding all the other ingredients.
3. Return the soup to a boil.
4. Add the solid ingredients to the jars, then top up with the liquid to within 1 inch of the neck.
5. Remove the air bubbles, clean the rims and add the lids and rings.
6. Place the jars in your canner and process for 75 minutes at 10 lbs psi for the weighted-gauge canner and 11 lbs psi for the dial-gauge canner at 0-1000ft elevation. Adjust pressure if you live at a higher altitude.
7. Allow to cool and lose pressure. Remove jars and set aside to cool overnight. Check seals, remove rings, label and store.

60. CHICKEN AND 16 BEAN SOUP

A soup packed full of protein for your family's health

Prep time: 10 minutes
Cook time: 2 hours
Makes: 6 pints

Ingredients

- 1kg 16 bean combination (500g dry)
- 1 1/2 quart of water
- 4 chicken breasts (cut into cubes)
- 8 cups of chicken broth/stock

Method

1. Prepare your canner and jars and keep the jars hot until use.
2. Put the beans in a pot and cover them with water and bring them to a

boil and turn off the heat. Leave them to soak for an hour. Then recover with water and cook for a further 30 minutes.

3. In another pot pour in the stock and bring to a simmer.
4. Turn up the heat to medium underneath your canner.
5. Fill ¼ of each jar with just the beans. Then add around 6 pieces of chicken to each jar and add more beans to bring it up to ¾. Pour in the broth until 1-inch from the top. Remove air bubbles and top up if necessary.
6. Clean the jar rims and place on the lids and rings.
7. Process in your canner for 75 minutes ensuring it is at the correct pressure for your canner and the altitude.
8. Once processed and jars are removed, leave them to cool overnight.
9. Check the seals, remove the rings, label and store.

61. LENTIL & CHICKEN SOUP

A protein-rich soup packed full of vitamins to give you a boost.

Prep: 30 minutes Process time: 75 minutes

Makes: 5 pints

Ingredients Listed as per quantity required for each jar

- 1/4 cup dry lentils
- 1/3 cup kale (chopped)
- Chicken broth (hot)
- ½ cup tomatoes (diced)
- 3 tbsp carrots (sliced thinly)
- 2 tbsp onions (diced)
- 3 jalapeno slices
- ½ tsp salt

Method

1. In each jar layer all the ingredients and fill up with warm chicken broth to ¾ inch from the top.
2. Wipe the rims and place on the lids and rings
3. Place the jars in your canner and process for 75 minutes at 10 psi for the weighted-gauge canner and 11 lbs psi for the dial-gauge canner at

0-1,000ft elevation. Adjust pressure according to your altitude. Allow the canner to cool and lose pressure before removing the jars.

4. Leave the jars on one side for 24 hours to set. Check the seals, remove the lids, and store them in your pantry.

62. ESSENTIAL CHICKEN SOUP

A family favorite that's a must-have in your pantry store.

Prep time: 1 hour 35 minutes
Cook time: 10 minutes
Makes: 4 pints

Ingredients

- 1 ½ cups of cooked chicken(diced)
- 2 quarts chicken stock
- ¾ cup carrots (sliced)
- ¾ cup celery (chopped)
- ½ cup onion (chopped)
- 1 ½ chicken bouillon cubes
- Salt
- Pepper

Method

1. Prepare your canner and warm the jars ready for your soup as per the manufacturer's instructions.
2. Combine all the ingredients in a large pot and bring them to a boil. Then simmer for 10 minutes.
3. Then, transfer the solid ingredients to the jars and then top up with the broth leaving 1-inch headspace.
4. Place on lids and rings and process in your canner for 75 minutes adjusting the pressure for your specific canner and your altitude.
5. Once processed, allow the canner to cool and lose pressure. Remove the jars and allow them to cool overnight.
6. Check the seals, remove the rings, label and store. Can last up to 18 months in your pantry.

63. MEXICAN CHICKEN SOUP

Prep/cook time: 4 hours 30 minutes

Makes: 8 servings

Ingredients

- 4 chicken breasts (cooked and cubed)
- 1 onion (chopped)
- 2 cups celery
- 1 ½ cups carrots (sliced)
- 2 14 oz cans of tomatoes
- 2 15 oz cans kidney beans (drained)
- 4 cups tomatoes (diced)
- 6 cups chicken broth
- 6 cups water
- 3 cups corn
- 3 chicken bouillon cubes
- 3 garlic cloves (crushed)
- 1 tsp ground cumin
- 1 tbsp canning salt

Method

1. Prepare your pressure canner and heat the jars.
2. Put all the ingredients in a pot apart from the chicken, bring to a boil, cover and simmer for 3 minutes. Then add the chicken and boil gently.
3. Pour the hot soup into the jars leaving a 1-inch headspace. Remove any air bubbles and top up if necessary. Attach the lids and bands and put them in the canner.
4. Process for 75 minutes adjusting the pressure according to the canner and the altitude.
5. Once the canner has cooled and lost its pressure, remove the jars and set them aside for 24 hours to cool. Check the seals, remove the bands, label them, and store them.

64. CHICKEN AND RED PEPPER SOUP

A soup packed full of flavor.

Prep time: 40 minutes
Processing time: 75 minutes
Makes: 7 pints

Ingredients

- 3 ½ lb chicken (diced)
- 7 garlic cloves (crushed)
- 5 ½ cups chicken broth
- 4 red peppers (seeded and diced)
- 2-3 oz sun-dried tomatoes
- 1 large onion (diced)
- 1 tbsp olive oil (divide)
- 2 tsp salt (divide)
- ½ tsp black pepper (divided)
- ½ tbsp onion powder
- 1 tsp garlic powder
- 1 bay leaf (in 4 pieces)

Method

1. Preheat the oven to 375 degrees F/190 degrees C. Prepare your canner and jars. Bring the canner to a simmer.
2. On an oven tray place the peppers with ½ tbsp olive oil, ¼ tsp black pepper, and ½ tsp salt and bake in the oven for 20 minutes.
3. In a pot put the onions and garlic with the remaining oil and cook on low heat. Add the peppers and sun-dried tomatoes. Puree the mixture until smooth and add some of the broth. Put it back in the pot and add the remaining broth. Adding the rest of the ingredients bring to a boil and reduce to simmer for 10 minutes.
4. Add the chicken to the jars to half full, topping with broth leaving 1-inch headspace. Remove the air bubbles and top up, if necessary, Clean the rims, add the lids and bands and place the jars in the canner.
5. Process for 75 minutes

65. CHICKEN TORTILLA SOUP

A delicious soup full of spice for your family to enjoy.

Process time: 75 minutes
Makes: 5 pints

Ingredients

- 2 chicken breasts
- 8 Roma tomatoes (diced)
- ½ large onion (diced)
- 3 cups chicken stock
- 2 cups corn kernels
- 1 cup dried black beans
- ¾ cup carrots (sliced)
- 1 cup water
- ½ cup mild green chilies (chopped)
- 3 garlic cloves, minced
- 1-2 dried cayenne peppers
- 1 tbsp canning gel
- ½ tbsp ground cumin
- ½ tbsp ground chili powder
- ½ tbsp sea salt
- ½ tsp oregano
- ½ tsp paprika

Method

1. Cook the chicken in a pot covered with 2 inches of water. Boil for 15 minutes. Remove, allow to cool, and cut up into chunks.
2. Wash the beans and boil them for 15 minutes if you wish to have a softer bean in your soup.
3. In a pot add all the ingredients, bring to a boil for 3 minutes, then add the chicken. Bring back to boil for 5 minutes then remove from heat. Remove and throw away the cayenne peppers.
4. Fill the jars to halfway with the soup, then add the broth leaving a 1-inch headspace. Remove any air bubbles and top up if necessary. Clean the rims and 'add the lids and rings and process in your canner for 75 minutes. Adjust the pressure according to your canner and your altitude.

66. TURKEY SOUP

A soup to enjoy any time or especially at thanksgiving.

Prep time: 10 minutes
Cook time: 2 hours
Makes: 10 servings

Ingredients

- 16 cups chicken stock
- 4 cups turkey (cubed)
- 1 cup carrots (sliced)
- 1 cup celery (chopped)
- 1 cup onion (chopped)
- Chicken bouillon
- Salt and pepper to taste

Method

1. In a pot mix all the ingredients and bring to a boil.
2. Prepare your canner and warm the jars in the canner whilst the soup is cooking.
3. Transfer the soup to the jars leaving 1-inch headspace. Remove any air bubbles and top up if necessary. Clean the rims and put on the lids and rings.
4. Place the jars in your canner and process for 75 minutes for pint jars at 10 lbs psi for a weighted-gauge canner and 11 lbs psi for a dial-gauge canner. Adjust the pressure if you are living at higher altitudes.
5. Allow the canner to cool and lose pressure, wait for 10 minutes, then remove the jars and leave to cool for 12-24 hours.
6. Check seals, remove the rings, label and store.

67. BEAN AND SAUSAGE SOUP

A tasty filling soup, packed with goodness to enjoy with the family. Delicious served with warm bread.

Prep time: 30 minutes
Cook time: 15 minutes
Makes: 7 pints

Ingredients

- ¾ cup pinto beans (dried)
- 1 lb Italian sausage
- ¾ cup black beans (dried)
- ¾ cup onion(diced)
- ½ cup celery(chopped)
- 1 cup carrot (peeled and sliced)
- 2 garlic cloves
- 4 cups beef bone stock
- 2 cups water
- ½ bunch kale (just the leaves, chopped)
- 1 tbsp olive oil
- 1 bay leaf
- ¼ tsp salt
- 1/8 tsp black pepper

Method

1. Clean and rinse the dried beans, ensuring they are of good quality going into your soup.
2. In a pot add the beans along with water to cover the beans by 2 inches and bring to a boil. Then cover and simmer for 30 minutes. Scoop out ½ cup of the liquid and put it on one side. Then drain the beans.
3. In another heat the oil and add the garlic, celery, and onion, and fry for around 5 minutes until the onions are clear. Add the sausage and cook.
4. Add the stock, bay leaf, water, carrots, and seasoning, and bring to a boil. Reduce to a simmer for 5 minutes, adding the beans, the ½ cup of bean liquid that you put on one side, and the kale. Mix well and cook for another 5 minutes. Take off the heat.
5. Ladle the solid mixture into your jars to ¾ full and top up with the liquid,

leaving the 1-inch headspace. Remove the air bubbles and top up if necessary.

6. Clean the rims, add the lids and rings and place them in your canner. Process for 75 minutes at 10 psi for a weighted-gauge canner and 11 lbs psi for a dial-gauge canner. Adjust pressure if you are at a different altitude to 0-1000ft.

7. Allow the canner to cool and lose pressure. Remove jars and leave to cool overnight. Check seals, remove rings, label, and store in your pantry.

68. SAUSAGE, POTATO, AND KALE SOUP

A tasty treat for all the family that will certainly satisfy their hunger.

Prep time: 40 minutes
Cook time: 1 hour 30 minutes
Makes: 7 pints

Ingredients

- 1 ½ lb sausage (ground)
- 3 ½ lbs potatoes (peeled and cubed)
- ½ lb kale
- 5 cups water
- 1 tbsp salt
- 1 tsp black pepper

Method

1. Brown the sausage in a pot, wash the vegetables, and prepare the potatoes. Once the sausage is cooked, add the vegetables to the pot and cover with water. Bring up to a boil and simmer for 10 minutes.

2. Prepare your canner and warm the jars.

3. Transfer the soup into the jars leaving 1-inch headspace. Add the solid first so each jar has an even amount.

4. Clean the rims, add the lids and bands, and process for 1 hour 30 minutes. Chose the correct pressure, depending on your canner and your altitude.

5. Allow the canner to cool and lose pressure before removing the jars.

6. Leave them to cool overnight. Check the seals, remove the bands, label them, and store them.

69. PORK TUSCAN SOUP

With additional spices, this delicious soup is filling and flavorsome.

Prep time: 10 minutes
Cook time: 2 hours
Makes: 4 pints

Ingredients

- 1 ½ lbs ground pork
- 2 large potatoes (peeled and cubed)
- ½ bunch kale (washed and blanched)
- 6 pints pork stock
- 2 garlic cloves (crushed)
- 1 small onion (diced)
- 1/8 tsp red pepper flakes
- 1 tsp salt
- 1 tsp pepper
- 1 tsp oregano

Method

1. Prepare your canner and warm the jars ready.
2. In a pan fry the pork add the seasonings and separately heat the stock.
3. Fill equally the jars with onion and garlic mix, followed by a small portion of kale and potatoes.
4. Then share the pork amongst the jars to ¾ full. Add the stock, leaving the 1-inch headspace. Remove the air bubbles and top up if necessary.
5. Clean the rims of the jars and place on the lids and the rings. Place the jars on the base of the canner. Process for 75 minutes, following the guidelines for correct pressure, according to your canner and altitude.
6. Cool the jars overnight and check the seals, remove the rings, label and add them to your store.

70. VENISON STEWED SOUP

A hearty warming soup

Prep time: 15 minutes
Cook time: 7 hours
Makes: 6 servings

Ingredients

- 1 lb venison (cut into chunks)
- 1 can of mixed vegetables
- ½ can potato slices
- ½ quart tomatoes (chopped)
- ½ can creamed corn
- ½ can tomato soup
- ½ onion(chopped)
- 1 can of green beans
- ½ tsp Worcestershire sauce
- ½ tsp salt
- 1/8 tsp black pepper

Method

1. First place the meat in a pan to brown and then combine all the ingredients with the meat in a large pot and cook on high heat for 5-7 hours.
2. Transfer the mixture to your jars, leaving 1-inch headspace. Remove any air bubbles. Clean the rims and place on the lids and rings.
3. Process the jars in your canner for 75 minutes at 10 psi for weighted-gauge canners and 11 lbs psi for dial-gauge canners.
4. Allow the canner to cool and lose pressure. Wait 10 minutes before removing the lid and taking out the jars. Allow the jars to rest for 24 hours. Check the seals, remove the rings, label them, and store them in your pantry.

71. RABBIT VEGETABLE SOUP

A healthy and tasty soup to prepare for your family.

Process time: 75 minutes
Makes: 4 pints

Ingredients

- 2 cups rabbit (chopped)
- 1 cup carrot (sliced)
- ½ cup onion (sliced)
- ½ cup celery (chopped)
- 1 ¾ quarts chicken stock or rabbit stock
- ½ tbsp garlic (crushed)
- ½ tsp basil
- ½ tsp salt
- ¼ tsp pepper

Method

1. Prepare your canner and 4-pint jars.
2. Put all the ingredients in a large pot and simmer for around 20 minutes.
3. Transfer the rabbit and vegetables to the jars, filling them halfway, and then top up with the broth/stock, leaving 1-inch headspace.
4. Add put all the lids and rings on the jars and process in your canner for 75 minutes. Adjust the pressure according to your canner and level of altitude. Once removed leave the jars to cool for 24 hours before checking the seals, removing the rings, labelling, and storing.

72. PHEASANT STOCK

This recipe can also apply to making stock from turkeys, partridge, goose, rabbit, and many more.

Prep time: 20 minutes
Cook time: 8 hours
Makes: 6 pints

Ingredients

- 3 pheasant carcasses

- 1 ½ carrots (chopped)
- 2 celery stalks (chopped)
- ½ bunch parsley stalks (chopped)
- 2 bay leaves
- ½ onion (chopped)
- 1 ½ tbsp sunflower oil
- 2 garlic cloves
- ½ tbsp peppercorns
- 1 tsp dried thyme
- Salt (to taste)

Method

1. Heat an oven to 400 degrees F/204.4 degrees. Place the pheasant in a pan coated with oil and salt and roast for around an hour or until dark brown.
2. Fill a pot 2/3 full of cold water, crush the pheasant, and add to the pot heat over a medium flame. Pour some water into the roasting tin.
3. The loose pieces in the roasting tin can then be added to the pot. Bring the pot up to a simmer and leave covered for 4 hours.
4. Then add all the rest of the ingredients and cook for another 1 ½ to 2 hours.
5. Strain and season to taste.
6. Transfer the stock to your jars and pressure can following your manufacturer's guidelines. This canned stock can last up to 2 years.

73. SHRIMP STOCK

Process time: 1 hour 20 minutes
Makes: 4 pints

Ingredients

- 2 ½ lbs shrimp shells
- ½ cup mushrooms (finely sliced)
- 1 cup onion (chopped)
- 1 cup celery (chopped)
- 1 cup carrots (chopped)
- 2 ½ quarts and 1 cup cold water
- 1 tbsp garlic (crushed)

- 1 bay leaf
- ¼ tsp dried thyme
- ¼ tsp black peppercorns
- 4 parsley stems

Method

1. Rinse the shells well and put them in a pot with all the ingredients. Bring up to a boil, then reduce to a simmer for 45 minutes to 1 hour. Skim any residual on the surface.
2. When cooked strain the liquid and cool using an ice bath.
3. Fill your jars with the liquid leaving a 1-inch headspace and process for 1 hour 20 minutes at the psi relating to your altitude and canner.
4. Allow to cool, check the seals, label them, and store them in your pantry.

74. BEEF BROTH

Prep time: 45 minutes
Cook time: 4 hours
Makes: 7 pints

Ingredients

- 3 lbs beef stock bones
- 2 onions (chopped)
- 2 carrots (chopped)
- 1 ½ celery sticks (chopped)
- ½ garlic
- 1 gallon water
- 1 bay leaf
- ½ tsp dried thyme
- ½ tsp dried rosemary
- ½ tsp dried parsley
- 5 peppercorns

Method

1. Preheat oven to 450 degrees F/232 degrees C.
2. Roast the beef bones in a roasting tin for 45 minutes. Move them to a pot with any bits from the bottom of the roasting pan.

3. Add the vegetables and flavorings to the pot and cover it with 2 inches of water.
4. Bring up to a boil and simmer for 4 hours. Strain the contents of the stockpot.
5. Prepare your canner and warm the jars inside. Ladle the broth to your jars leaving 1-inch headspace. Add the lids and rings, wipe the rims, and process in your canner.
6. It will require 20 minutes at 10 psi for the weighted-gauge canner and 11 lbs psi for your dial-gauge canner.
7. Allow the jars to cool for 12-24 hours, check the seals, remove the rings, label, and store for up to 18 months.

75. PORK STOCK

A stock that is used in many recipes, particularly Asian recipes therefore great to have to hand.

Process time: 25 minutes

Ingredients
- Pork bones
- Water

Method
1. Preheat an oven to 350 degrees F/176.6 degrees C and roast the bones for around 45 minutes.
2. In a stock pot add the bones to the water in a ratio of 1/3 to 2/3.
3. Ensure the bones are covered with water and simmer gently for around 12 hours to maintain the flavor of the stock.
4. Strain the stock and fill the jars, leaving 1-inch headspace. Your canner will require around 2 inches of boiling water in its base.
5. Process in your canner for 25 minutes at 10 lbs psi with a weighted-gauge canner and 11 lbs psi for a dial-gauge canner. Once cooled check the seals, remove the rings, label and store.

76. CHICKEN STOCK

A useful stock used in many recipes.

Prep time: 30 minutes
Cook time: 5 hours
Makes: 4 pints

Ingredients

- 2 ½ lbs chicken bones
- 1 ½ garlic cloves (crushed)
- 1 onion(sliced)
- 1 carrot (chopped)
- 1 celery stalk(chopped)
- 1 bay leaf
- 4 peppercorns
- 2 ½ quarts water
- ½ tsp dried parsley
- ¼ tsp dried rosemary

Method

1. Preheat the oven to 425 degrees F/218.3 degrees C and place the chicken bones in a roasting tin, covering them with the celery, carrots, onions, and garlic.
2. Roast for 45 minutes approximately until the bones have browned.
3. Transfer contents to a pot and any remains in the roasting tin.
4. Add the herbs, peppercorns, bay leaf, and enough water to cover the bones by 2 inches and bring the pot to a boil, then reduce to simmer for 4 hours.
5. Remove the vegetables and the meat from your stock, strain the liquid and allow to cool overnight. Remove the fat from the surface. Return the stock to a large pot and bring it to a boil.
6. Prepare your canner and warm the jars inside by half-filling them with hot water and allowing the pressure canner to simmer.
7. Fill the jars with the hot stock leaving the 1-inch headspace. Remove the air bubbles, add the lids and bands and return to the canner and bring it to a boil. Process the jars at 10 lbs psi for 20 minutes. Adjust pressures according to your altitude.

8. Remove and allow to cool for 12-24 hours. Check the seals, remove the rings, wash, label, and store them in your pantry. Use within one year.

77. TURKEY STOCK

A versatile stock to use with different meals.

Prep time: 1 hour
Cook time: 25 minutes

Ingredients

- Turkey (carcass and bones)
- Water
- Salt

Method

1. Remove the meat from the turkey carcass and either roast it in the oven for an hour or place it in a pot and cover it with water and bring it to a boil, then reduce it to a simmer for 45 minutes.
2. Strain the mixture and leave it in the fridge overnight.
3. Remove any excess fat from the stock and reheat it in a pot.
4. Pour the liquid into your pint jars leaving 1-inch headspace. Clean the rims of the jars, put on the lids and rings, and process in your canner. Process for 20 minutes at 10 lbs psi for weighted-gauge and 11 lbs psi for the dial-gauge canner.
5. Allow the canner to cool and lose pressure, leave for 10 minutes, then remove the jars from the canner and set aside to cool for 12-24 hours.
6. Check seals, remove the rings, label and store.

CHAPTER 9
SOUP & SAUCE BASE RECIPES FOR ANY MEAT

78. TOMATO SAUCE BASE

Prep time: 20 minutes
Cook time: 4 hours
Makes: 8 pints

Ingredients

- 16 lbs tomatoes (chopped into large pieces)
- 4 cups of onion (diced)
- 2 cup celery (diced)
- 12 bay leaves
- 2 cups fresh parsley
- ½ cup sugar (optional)
- 1 tsp black pepper
- 5 tsp salt

Method

1. In a large pot add the tomatoes, bay leaves, parsley, celery, and onion. Cook gently until soft. Sieve the mixture and put 4 cups of puree on one side to cool.
2. Add seasoning and bring to a boil.
3. Transfer to your jars, leaving 1-inch headspace. Clean the rims, add lids and rings, and put them in your pressure canner. Process at 10 lbs psi for a weighted-gauge canner and 11 lbs psi for a dial-gauge canner for 25 minutes.
4. Remove your jars once the canner has cooled and lost its pressure. Set the jars to one side to cool.
5. Check seals, remove rings, label and store.

6. When using your soup heat up with an equal amount of either water, milk, or chicken broth.

79. VEGETABLE BROTH

Prep time: 5 minutes
Cook time: 2 hours

Ingredients

- 2-3 carrots
- 1 onion
- 3-4 celery sticks
- 8 oz mushrooms (chopped)
- 1 tbsp dried thyme
- 1 bay leaf
- 1 tsp black peppercorns

Method

1. Wash and prepare all your vegetables and add them to a large pot along with water leaving 2 inches of headspace. Add the seasonings and simmer for two hours.
2. Prepare your canner and warm the jars ready for your broth.
3. Remove the vegetables and strain the liquid.
4. Fill your prepared warm jars with the broth leaving 1-inch headspace.
5. Clean the rims and place a lid and ring on the jars and process them for 20 minutes (for pints) at the pressure relating to your elevation and canner.
6. Once processed leave the jars to cool for 24 hours, check seals, remove rings, label and store.

80. SPICY VEGETABLE, CORN AND TOMATO SOUP BASE

Prep time: 45 minutes
Cook time: 1 hour 30 minutes
Makes: 6 pints

Ingredients

- 5 cups tomatoes (chopped)
- ¼ cup hot pepper (seeded and chopped)
- 2/3 cup green bell pepper (seeded and chopped)
- 2/3 cup red pepper (chopped)
- 2/3 cup onion (chopped)
- 2/3 cup carrot (peeled and sliced)
- 4 cups whole kernel corn (uncooked)
- 1 ½ cups water
- 3 ¼ cups tomato juice
- ¾ tbsp hot sauce
- 1 ¼ tsp chili powder
- 1 ¼ tsp ground cumin
- ¾ tsp cayenne pepper
- ¾ tsp ground black pepper
- ¾ tsp salt

Method

1. Prepare your canner and jars.
2. In a large pot add the tomatoes, onions, carrots, peppers, and corn.
3. Add all the remaining ingredients and bring to a boil. Reduce to simmer for 15 minutes.
4. Fill each jar with the solid mixture to ¾ full and top up with the liquid, leaving 1-inch headspace.
5. Remove any air bubbles and top up if necessary. Clean the rims of the jars and place on the lids and rings.
6. Process in your canner at 10 lbs psi for weighted gauge canner for 60 minutes at 0-1,000ft altitude. Process at 11 lbs for dial-gauge canner for the same duration. Alter pressures if you live at a higher altitude.

CLAIM YOUR AMAZING FREE BONUS

**With This QR Code or go to
https://drive.google.com/drive/u/0/
folders/1ptYfs25TjhhAORppRjdfcUCTW5KBk8hQ**

Made in the USA
Monee, IL
02 September 2024

65024510R00059